WINGS OF THE MORNING

Flight and Faith in War and Peace

by

Jon R. Harris

May 15th, 2006

Linda and Bill,

Thank you for your interest in "Wings of the Morning." I trust that you'll read it as a metaphor of the trials and struggles of life, but always with the grace and the glory of God shining through it all.

"Those who hope in the Lord...
will soar on wings as eagles."
Isaiah 40:13 NIV

John R Harris

CONTENTS

INTRODUCTION

Whenever I've been asked during my life, "Where are you from?," my stock reply, which invariably draws at least a smile, is, "Nowhere."

You see, my dad was military as I was growing up, and then my own military career began at the Naval Academy at Annapolis, Maryland when I was still seventeen. I had traveled extensively as a child and continued to travel equally as extensively during my young adult years after my Academy days.

As one of the last of the pre-WWII babies, I was born in San Pedro, California in August of 1941, just a couple of months prior to the Japanese attack on Pearl Harbor. Early in 1942 my mother moved my 18-month-older brother and me up to Bremerton, Washington, where my dad and the rest of the crew of the *USS Nevada* were ultimately sent during the months it took for the *Nevada*, the only battleship to get underway during the attack, to be raised, repaired, and refitted.

During the next eleven years my family lived in the four corners of the nation, from Bremerton, Washington, to Boston, Massachusetts, and from Key West, Florida, to Long Beach, California, and in various places in between. We finally ended up in San Francisco for my dad's retirement from the navy.

After his retirement, our family settled in Pineville, Louisiana, a small town across the Red River from where my dad had been a navy recruiter in Alexandria. Since he was known by every high school principal in a hundred-mile radius and planned to get a teaching degree in college, he felt that this would be the ideal place for us to settle.

He further realized that Pineville contained the three items he most desired for his retirement, a local college where he could attain that teaching degree, a local golf course where he could play golf to his heart's content after completing his degree and finding a teaching position, and a moderately-sized high school which would allow his two sons to be challenged to the extent of their abilities in all areas and still be able to excel where possible.

Thus, Pineville, Louisiana became "home" for me. I spent my junior high and high school years there, and ultimately that's where both my mom and dad are buried.

My high school career was very good to me. I enjoyed and did well in both academics and athletics. Coincidentally, I was both a tri-captain of the football team and a tri-valedictorian of my graduating class.

But it was as I entered the U.S. Naval Academy on July 7, 1959 that I discovered the environment for which I was made. I loved virtually every minute and was awed by virtually every facet of my time there. And in so many ways I was there at the right time, and often in the right place at the right time.

For example, I had the privilege of raising the first fifty-star flag over New York City on July 4th, 1960, while on my "Youngster Cruise" (a two-month cruise in the summer between a midshipman's fourth class and third class years). The states of Alaska and Hawaii had been accepted into the Union in 1959, and President Eisenhower had decreed that a new, fifty-star design should be raised over the United States on the Fourth of July, 1960. The first flag to be unfurled over the nation was at Fort McHenry in Baltimore, Maryland, the site of the composition of *The Star-Spangled Banner*, at 12:01 AM on the Fourth. Then another midshipman and I along with two West Point cadets raised the second flag over the nation (we were told) and the first over the city at twelve noon atop a building in the center of the financial district of NYC to a great deal of pomp and circumstance at street level below us.

As well, during my four years at Navy, I was among the third of the Brigade that marched in John F. Kennedy's inaugural parade in January of 1961, my class was one of the three classes which were at the Academy when *both* of Navy's Heisman Trophy winners, Joe Bellino and Roger Staubach, played for Navy, I began an ongoing, forty-five year association with the Officer's Christian Fellowship, a worldwide organization that ministers to military personnel and their families, the protestant members of the Brigade of Midshipmen elected me to be the president of the Naval Academy Christian Association, and I graduated tenth in my class of 890 midshipmen.

Having met my bride-to-be as a third classman (sophomore) in the fall of 1960, we married the day after my June 5th graduation in 1963. Being a "Bachelor for a Day" (midshipmen cannot marry while at the Academy) was enough bachelorhood for me, and so my nineteen-year-old bride accompanied this young twenty-one-year-old navy Ensign to flight training at Pensacola, Florida. That began what would be the foundation of many of the defining moments of my adult life, my aviation career. Fifteen months later I received my Wings of Gold, signifying that I was now, indeed, a Naval Aviator.

During the next eight years, I grew up. I was faced with war, with fear, and with extreme challenges to the limits of my personal capabilities and internal resources. I learned to perform in spite of the fear and to accomplish my duties to the best of my abilities in the face of dangers I could never have anticipated. And I learned most of all that my faith in

God through Jesus Christ was the foundation and central core of my life...or it wasn't really faith at all.

Through life-or-death situations in which death was a certainty without quick action, good fortune, or just plain miraculous intervention; through the types of events that all pilots face in one way or another that either kill them or make them wiser and allow them to get older; through flights of fancy and flights of pure terror, I faced my humanity and my mortality. In this book, I have recounted the events as best as I can remember them, without embellishment and without fanfare, with one purpose in mind. That purpose is to demonstrate in one individual's life how God can meet us in every aspect and every venue of life, how His constant care can bear us up through tragedy, through soul-gripping dread, and through the excitement, the joy, and the adventure of life.

Some of the narratives in this book simply convey what I personally gained through the aviation event I experienced; in others I use real-life happenings to demonstrate, to illustrate, or to allegorize spiritual or biblical principles. I trust that the adventurous "fluff" will not obscure the value and depth of the spiritual truths explored and explained.

So I invite you to "come fly with me" as we take the "wings of the morning" unto "the uttermost parts of the sea."

Jon R. Harris

DEDICATION *for*
"WINGS OF THE MORNING"

This book is dedicated to
"FREEDOM"

*T*o the national and personal freedom and the freedom of conscience of each citizen as was envisioned by the founders of this nation, for which cause they concluded their formal assertion of that freedom in the "Declaration of Independence" with this extraordinary covenant, *"And for the support of this Declaration, with a firm reliance on the protection of Divine Providence, we mutually pledge to each other our Lives, our Fortunes, and our sacred Honor."* Many lost their lives; most lost their fortunes; none lost their sacred honor.

To the freedom of spirit for which Patrick Henry advocated in his eloquent defense of the use of force to gain that freedom before the Virginia House of Delegates in March of 1775, *"Is life so dear or peace so sweet as to be purchased at the price of chains and slavery? Forbid it, Almighty God! I know not what course others may take; but as for me, give me liberty, or give me death!"*

To the freedom sustained for each of us throughout this nation's history by the valiant men and women of our military forces, who have understood that there are causes greater than "self" that are fully worth the laying down of one's life. This is so poignantly demonstrated in a Civil War letter from Major Sullivan Ballou in July of 1861 to his wife a week before his death: *"I have sought most closely and diligently, and often in my breast, for a wrong motive in thus hazarding the happiness of those I loved and I could not find one. A pure love of my country and of the principles I have often advocated before the people and "the name of honor that I love more than I fear death" have called upon me and I have obeyed. Sarah, my love for you is deathless, it seems to bind me to you with mighty cables that nothing but Omnipotence could break; and yet my love of Country comes over me like a strong wind and bears me irresistibly on with all these chains to the battlefield."*

And finally to the most precious freedom of all, the overflowing and eternal freedom of the soul, which has been provided by the Christ who promised that, *"You shall know the truth, and the truth shall make you free. If therefore the Son shall make you free, you shall be free indeed,"* (John 8:32 and 36 NASB). He then disclosed to His disciples the source of that truth that should set us free by revealing, *"I am the way, and the truth, and the life; no one comes to the Father, but through Me,"* (John 14:6 NASB). And, later the Apostle Paul affirmed in Galatians 5:1 (NIV), *"It is for freedom that Christ has set us free."*

I thank God constantly for the privilege of drinking deeply from these cascading springs of liberty, which energize the heart of this nation and nourish its people. We have been so blessed by God.

1.

THIS TREASURE IN CLAY JARS…
STRUCK DOWN, BUT NOT DESTROYED

If I ascend up into heaven, thou art there;
If I make my bed in hell, behold, thou art there.
Psalm 139:8 KJV

"PILOTS, MAN YOUR AIRCRAFT."

The traditional call to "mount up" for carrier pilots ever since there has been naval aviation blared over the ship's 1MC. The scheduled pilots had just completed the general briefing for the full attack force that was to make the first major strike of the Vietnam War into Hanoi, North Vietnam. The date was September 20, 1965.

The four of us from VA-72, having returned to our ready room for our squadron briefing and to suit up, grabbed our flight helmets and headed toward the ready room door. I had just stepped out into the corridor and was about to close the door, when the 1MC sounded again.

"All Ready Rooms, this is CAG…I forgot to mention that there will be a helo on a cruiser off the coast in case anyone should need it."

One more step and I wouldn't have heard that…one more step and I would have ended that day as a Prisoner of War, for the next seven and a half years.

My name is Jon Harris. At the time about which I am writing, I was two years out of the U. S. Naval Academy (Class of '63), I had married the day after graduation, I had recently completed my flight-training program, and I was now the junior pilot of my squadron, VA-72 (Aviation Attack Squadron Seventy-Two) flying the A-4E Skyhawk. We were assigned to Air Wing 7, based out of Virginia Beach, Virginia, now embarked in the *USS INDEPENDENCE* (CVA 62) and deployed as the first east-coast-based aircraft carrier to the war in Vietnam. We arrived and began combat flight operations on July 1, 1965, just in time for Independence Day. Ironically enough, we completed our tour on the line on November 11th...Veteran's Day.

Lt(jg) Jon R. Harris – September, 1965
(Photo by Bob Wilson)

The attack I was about to participate in was an Alpha Strike (a major attack) to be coordinated with our sister carrier on the line, the *USS Midway*. Our strike force was to attack a highway and railroad bridge leading north out of Hanoi, which was a major supply route for incoming supplies from the North's allies. The Midway's air wing was to hit an airbase southeast of the city in order to preclude the bad guys from launching MiG interceptors at our formation.

As we approached the city at 20,000 feet, the first of some twenty surface-to-air missiles (SAM 2s) fired during the attack streaked across in front of the formation and exploded near the lead aircraft. This was the beginning of the first major guided missile counter-attack in history. Fortunately the lead aircraft was not hit, but the Air Group Commander (CAG) who was leading the attack shouted into his radio, "Hit the deck!" This was designed to put us below the radar coverage of the radar-guided missiles.

We had briefed that, were the formation to be separated for any reason, we were to rendezvous at 500 feet around a reservoir southwest of the city. There were two problems with this. The first was that it subjected us to substantially more enemy ground fire, since small arms could be used as well as smaller caliber anti-aircraft batteries. The second was that CAG had failed to mention which way we were to fly around the reservoir. So trying not to be involved in "bumper cars" with the other aircraft became our first priority, since half were circling in a clockwise direction; the other half in a counterclockwise pattern. It was during this event that, even through the great turbulence caused by the heat rising from the ground, I felt something odd – a movement of the aircraft that was just…*different.*

But right at that time, the CAG called, "Decoy flight [our squadron's call sign], roll in!" That was our cue to climb to 12,000 feet, find the target and roll in to the 70-degree dive we had perfected to allow us minimum time in the dive, to drop our bombs at 7,000 and to be out by 4,000, which kept us above most of the AA fire.

Starting out from 500 feet with 3,000 pounds of armament strapped to the aircraft (six 500 lb. bombs) meant that the climb to 12K was excruciatingly slow – emotionally one of the slowest rides I'd ever taken. We were sitting ducks in our climb, but, fortunately, no one was hit. I found the target, made the dive, dropped on target, and pulled out, jinking back and forth, up and down to preclude radar-guided anti-aircraft guns from locking on. All the while I was turning toward the east to begin the high-speed run to the South China Sea and safety. Out there, even if a pilot were forced to eject from a damaged aircraft, we had air superiority over the water and, therefore, a rescue helicopter or destroyer could safely pick him up. Over land, he was as good as captured should he have to "punch out."

I joined up with an aircraft in our sister A-4 squadron from the *Independence*, and we checked each other's aircraft over for battle damage. Seeing none, he took the lead (since everybody was senior to me in both squadrons), and we headed out to "feet wet." About ten miles from the city, we spotted an A-6 Intruder going our way. The *Independence* had brought to the war the first operational A-6 squadron. (In fact, the pilot who spoke for the first returning POWs at Clark AFB in February 1973, then-Captain Jeremiah A. Denton, was the Executive Officer [second in command] of the A-6 squadron.)

Since the A-6s had electronic countermeasures against SAMs, we caught up with the A-6 and each tucked up under a wing. We finally felt good about our chances of getting back in one piece.

Just then I got one of the major shocks of my life! My "FIRE" warning light came on! I couldn't believe it – nothing was happening that I could tell…yet. I called on the other A-4 pilot to slide over and check me out. I moved away from the

A-6, and the A-4 joined up on my left side about 50 feet away. At that point I called the strike leader and told him, "CAG, this is Decoy Three-One-Three. I think I'm going to have to get out of my aircraft." I was told later that I said it so calmly that no one initially picked up on the *extremis* I was in. "Say again," he responded, and I repeated what I had said.

Then things began to deteriorate very rapidly in my cockpit. First I smelled what I thought was burning wire insulation coming through my oxygen mask. At that time, I experienced an instantaneous panic. I began saying to myself, "I've got to turn off the electricity! I've got to turn off the electricity!" And I began to look wildly around the cockpit for the "Off" switch for "the electricity." But, in an aircraft like mine, one didn't turn "the electricity" off. Every electrical component had its own "On/Off" switch.

But the panic only lasted a couple or three seconds, until I felt the rudder pedals "slip" – they each moved back just a short distance. However, that was enough.

Now I had three indications of a fire – the "FIRE" warning light, the smell of burning "something," and the obvious mechanical movement suggesting the fire had burnt through the hydraulic lines. I was in bad trouble…and it was just going to get worse!

Two things then happened simultaneously. I heard the other pilot say, "I've got you," and my plane began a rapid roll to the right. I slapped the stick hard twice to see if I could stop the roll. The stick was frozen! Without conscious thought (and from constant practice in case I ever needed to eject *right now*) I reached down between my knees and pulled the alternate ejection handle.

Boom! I was gone. The plane had rolled ninety degrees, and so I ejected horizontal to the ground. There was an eerie sensation of tumbling through some type of thick goo – I later said it felt like it was "gravy," the air seemed so thick at that airspeed. The other pilot told me he had looked at his altimeter just before this and saw that we were at 1200 feet over some mountains. I had seen that we were traveling at 400 knots (about 450 mph).

What I didn't know in all of this was that just after the other pilot said, "I've got you," he saw the back half of my aircraft burst into flame just aft of the cockpit and then separate from the front half. When the plane started the roll to the right, I was in fact, flying a "rock," something that had absolutely *no* aerodynamic capability. When he saw the flames, he screamed, "You're on fire! You're on fire! Eject! Eject!" I heard none of that, since I was already out of the aircraft.

When my parachute opened, instead of the "jerk" that many pilots complain of, I just noticed that all the terrific motion simply stopped...everything was quiet. As the chute opened my head did snap forward, and I saw the plane burning on the ground. Later, a quick evaluation of the situation confirmed that I'd made exactly the right decision in ejecting when I did. Since it took 4.2 seconds from pulling the ejection handle to the opening of the chute (according to the ejection seat specs), and, because you couldn't eject safely out of an A-4 if it were inverted below 900 feet (because the parachute wouldn't open before you hit the ground), then I had somewhere between one and at the most two seconds to get out with the cockpit at ninety degrees to the horizon before it continued its roll to inverted and fell below the 900-foot level. *Any* delay of *any* kind for *any* reason would have been fatal.

As I began to gather my wits about me, it was very apparent that I truly was at the end of my...risers. The only thing I could think to say at that point was less an exclamation and more a plaintive invocation of the presence of the Almighty. "Oh, God!," I pensively whispered.

I looked around and saw that I was floating down into a bowl-shaped valley surrounded by mountains with a creek running through it from my left and in front of me to my back right. Directly off to the right was a village with some sort of movement in it. As I looked up at my canopy, I saw that a couple of the nylon cords attached to the risers were looped over it partially collapsing one side. With a little maneuvering I was able to correct that.

The thing that initially bothered me the most was that it didn't seem as though I was actually descending. I didn't know if air currents in this valley were rising or what, but it seemed like I was at the same altitude for the longest time. I learned later what was true then. The human eye cannot discern movement downward above a certain altitude. In fact, when you can finally perceive that you're really coming down, you're very close to landing.

I decided that I needed to do two things before I hit the ground...first, I wanted to steer the chute away from the village. Now we'd been taught in training that you simply pull down on the two risers on the side you want to direct the chute. What they didn't mention to us of was that, to try to do that, you are actually pulling yourself *up* the riser instead of pulling it down. (It might be noted here that this was a military issue circular parachute with no real direction-guidance capability). So, I pulled and tugged and fought with the chute for several minutes seemingly without success. But, it must have helped some, since I ultimately landed short and to the left of the village.

The second thing I wanted to do was to activate my personal radio, which as pilots we wore connected to the front of our survival vest. I quickly reached down and pulled the lanyard that removed a small ball that kept the radio from accidentally being turned on and draining the battery. But, in the stress and tension of the moment, I made a nearly fatal mistake. The ball was pulled only halfway out of its housing and, therefore, never allowed the radio to start its beeping. Since the other pilot was circling above me at about 10,000 feet, it wasn't a problem of not being found. It was a problem (as I found out later) of whether or not I was alive.

After what seemed to be an interminable time in the air, I began to notice that I was, in fact, coming down. Since I was descending into some sort of trees or bushes, I assumed the correct landing posture for going through trees. And then, as I quickly approached the trees, I prepared to hit the ground with slightly bent knees, ready to roll to the ground as we'd been taught in training.

But to my surprise, as I went through the undergrowth, I hit the ground and just stood there. My chute had caught up in the tops of the medium-sized trees (or *really* large bushes) and the cords and risers stretched just to the point that my feet hit the ground, but I couldn't fall over. So I quickly pushed up the quick-releases for the risers on my parachute harness and stepped out of the chute. Compulsively I looked at my watch – 12:29 PM.

Right then I clearly remember saying to myself that I had only one chance to get this right, and even then I was almost assuredly going to be captured. So, I quickly inventoried the survival gear from the ejection seat pan (which stayed hooked to me when the ejection seat itself separated as part of the ejection sequence) to see what would be of value to me. The main thing that I wanted was the extra batteries for the radio. I assumed that, at the end of the day, it would be communications which would assure me of rescue, should I, in fact, be fortunate enough to actually be rescued, that is.

One thing that I hadn't noticed yet but soon did was that the antenna on my radio had broken off during the descent through the trees. Not knowing the full capability of the radio, I was hoping (against hope) that it would still transmit and receive, at least at close range. That hope did not come true.

The next thing that I figured out was that it was necessary to get away from the parachute (which I couldn't get out of the trees), since it would be a beacon for whoever would be looking for me, good guys or bad. As well, I wanted to get away from the village. Remembering that last message CAG had passed on to us about the helo on the cruiser, I knew that I wanted to at least give them a chance to come in and get me. So I needed to get away from both the village and the parachute, but I didn't want to be too far away, so that if the rescue helo could find the chute they would know that I was in the area.

Thus I began a quick retreat from the direction of the village through the undergrowth. I intended to get to a clear area where the helo could come in and snatch me out of harm's way. But the more I ran through the undergrowth, the harder it became and the more tiring, much like those nightmares where you are fleeing 'something', but in slow motion and to no avail. After a while I looked behind me and saw that I was dragging half the forest along with me. Glancing down, I saw that I had branches, vines, and assorted other wild impediments twisted around something at both ankles.

On the left ankle was the bottom half of the kneepad we pilots strap on our leg above the knee and use for taking notes during our flight briefing and then for writing on during a flight, if that is necessary. The top half had been torn off during the ejection. Most right-handed pilots strap their kneepad on their right leg. I chose not to do that, since the kneepad hindered my ability to easily get to the alternate ejection handle with my right hand. So even though I had to reach across to my left leg to write whatever might be necessary, still being able to get to that ejection handle without fumbling around did prove to save my life.

On my right ankle was the machete that I'd purchased in the Philippines prior to our going into combat. About 15 inches long and in its own scabbard, my reason for having it on all my combat flights was for more than just personal defensive purposes. It was apparent that the jungles of Vietnam could be so dense as to not be passable without a means of cutting a pathway. So I had my squadron's parariggers to sew some elastic bands near the top and bottom of the scabbard so that I could strap it to the outside of my right calf. Reaching from the ankle to just below the knee, I felt comforted that I would have a multiuse tool available should I need it.

However, while running through the undergrowth on that particular Sunday, I had forgotten about the machete, and that's when I found that it had slipped down until it was scraping the ground and was picking up more forest-floor debris than it was missing.

Pausing to correct the situation, I unsnapped the kneeboard and tossed it; then I took the machete in its scabbard and slid it down against my chest in between my harness and my flight suit. In passing I noted that the force of the ejection had bottomed out the machete so powerfully on the deck of the cockpit that the last half inch or so at the pointed end was curled back on itself.

As I began climbing the increasingly steep slope of the mountain on the eastern side of the valley, I soon left trees and bushes and entered a growth of tall "elephant grass" which was about waist high. Unfortunately, as I continued to climb, I reached a point where I could see the village...which, of course, meant that anyone there could see me. So, that's where I decided to make my stand in order to have the chance to be rescued. Between me and the village I also could make out my parachute in the tops of the trees. If the good guys didn't get me first, there was no doubt that the bad guys would know precisely where to start looking.

While I was lying there in the tall grass trying to keep my wits about me, I decided to take off my heavy parachute harness and G-suit. To do so I had to unsnap my survival vest from the harness and to fix it up for wearing on its own. I did this by taking the shoulder straps of the survival vest out of their pockets in order to buckle them together. It was at that point that I realized just how much in shock I was. I looked at the strap and then looked at the buckle and looked at the strap and then at the buckle, back and forth several times wondering how the strap was supposed to be threaded through the buckle in order for it not to slip. I simply couldn't figure it out. I must have taken ten minutes to finally master the task. I knew then that I was working at no better than 75% mental capacity. That scared me. I certainly couldn't afford too many brain cramps like that and still hope to get out of the situation.

Just then, I quit breathing...for about the next thirty minutes. I had heard something or someone moving in the grass somewhere across the slope. I fingered my pistol, wondering if I could use it against a human being, unless, of course, it was in defense of my life. I just didn't know, but I did know that I wanted it handy in the event that using it would assist in my rescue.

In a few minutes it happened again. I pressed myself lower into the grass. I continued to refuse to breathe, fearing that the sound of the breathing would give away my position. But nothing else happened. No one appeared; there were no voices. About the third time I heard the rustling of leaves, soon after I noticed a welcome breeze drift over me. And a few minutes later, "rustle, rustle" and then the breeze. It took the entire half hour to figure out that there was a ravine about fifty to a hundred yards around the slope from my position, and a breeze would blow across the tops of some trees in the ravine that were barely visible to me; the breeze would then reach me. When I realized what was happening I finally felt that it was safe to breathe again. I was a bit hypoxic, but none the worse for the scare.

About that time a very strange sound broke the silence; it was the sound of an airplane, a propeller-driven airplane. He was one of us! He began circling the valley in his Al Skyraider about 200 feet higher than I was. His was a RESCAP mission (Rescue Combat Air Patrol). He was to try to find me and then to use his four powerful 20-millimeter cannons to keep the bad guys at bay with their heads down while the helo came in and did its thing (I hoped).

But, I felt caught between a couple of risky decisions. If I revealed my position visually to him, then the enemy might hone in on the visual display. But, if I didn't reveal my position, there would be a question as to whether the helo would even come in. I tried to call the pilot on my radio, but it didn't seem to be working...the loss of the aerial seemed to have fully disabled it. I was hoping that, should the helo actually arrive, it might fly close enough to me for us to be able to communicate. But right then I wasn't too concerned, for each time that the plane flew over my position, I could see the pilot looking down...so I waved to let him know I was OK and ready for pick up. It was not until I was back at the carrier that I found out what was really happening during that time.

As the A-1 driver circled, he was trying to determine if I was still stuck in the parachute...so he never saw me halfway up the mountain in the elephant grass. After several orbits, he finally radioed to the pilot of the helicopter, which was then just off the coast, "Don't come in...the pilot is either dead or unconscious in his chute." The helo pilot did a quick calculation of the fuel it would take to come to the position the A-1 pilot gave him for the parachute and decided that, if he left right away, he had just enough fuel to come in and get me and make it back to the cruiser. If he delayed any more at all, he needn't bother. So he chose to come in right then anyway, just on the off chance that I had escaped the parachute...bless him!

After a while, about an hour and a half after the shootdown, I heard the glorious and very distinctive "whop, whop, whop" of the helicopter coming from behind me over the mountain.

He flew directly over me, and I decided now was the time.

I keyed the radio and said, "Helo, Helo, this is the pilot on the ground…I'm at your six o'clock." As if on cue he started a turn. "Aha!" I thought to myself, "He can hear me!" So I kept giving him directions in his turn until he had circled around facing me. "I'm at your twelve o'clock!" I told him. But he continued the turn. Dejectedly I recognized that his turn had simply begun when he passed over the parachute. He wasn't hearing me at all.

As he circled once more I knew it was time to expose my position to the world. I had taken the day/night flares out of the seat pan when I retrieved the batteries for the radio. So I took one out of my pocket and grabbed the metal loop at the daylight end of the flare. (The daylight end produces a fluorescent orange smoke and the night end produces a bright flame.)

As the helo circled, turning to face me, I performed the lighting of the flare just as designed and taught in survival school; I held the flare in my left hand, grabbed the metal loop with my right forefinger and snapped it off with a quick jerk…except that it didn't come off! Stunned, I saw that the helo was continuing its turn. Quickly I tried again, and again, and again, tugging at the loop. When it finally came off and the smoke began to pour out of the end of the flare, all I could see of the helo was its tail and tail rotator flying away from me.

I stood there waving the flare to disperse the smoke more widely, all the while fearing that the helo would not turn in time to see it. Later I learned that the A-1 pilot had climbed to about 10,000 feet, and he was the one who saw the smoke and directed the helo back to me.

When I saw the helo turn back and head directly for me, I began waving the map of North Vietnam we'd been provided which had been in my survival vest. It was a plastic-coated map to keep it from deteriorating in the extreme humidity.

However, the map was of the whole of North Vietnam, so it was like having a map of Vermont and trying to find yourself on it after landing on a ridgeline somewhere in the northeastern sector of the state.

So the map's best value for me at that point was simply as a banner to help the pilots to see me. As I stood there, I was in fatigues (the only flight suits we had available to us on shipboard at that early phase of the war were orange, so we simply bought green fatigues from the base exchange and flew in them). I had a floppy camo hat in my survival vest that I had put on when I discarded my flight helmet, and I had my pistol in its holster and ammunition belt crisscrossed over my chest with the radio which was on a strap and which I had not yet discarded.

I was told later that the helo's aircrewman saw me as they approached and started yelling, "He's Vietcong! He's Vietcong! Don't pick him up!" Fortunately for me, the pilot and copilot were a mite cooler under pressure, and they had more confidence that I was the good guy they'd come in to rescue.

I anticipated that when they reached me they would hover and lower the retrieval apparatus, most likely the "horse collar," a device at the end of the retrieval line that allowed the person being rescued to place the device around his torso and up under his arms and then to hold onto it for dear life as he is winched up into the helo. But, when they approached me, they didn't even slow down, just continued up over the mountain behind me. Now I was confused.

Were they going to approach me from a different direction? Did they want me to climb to the top of the mountain so that the helo could land and I could board that way? I just didn't know. But I thought that the latter possibility had more credence.

So I began to climb, and I found out two very disturbing facts. One was that, the higher I climbed in the elephant grass, the more dead grass was piled up under the live shoots. After just a little while, it really felt as though I was trying to climb in knee-deep mud! And secondly I found that the shock I was still experiencing plus the high-speed ejection having wrenched my body and banged up my legs simply rendered me physically incapable of making that climb that day.

So I just sat down to wait, hoping that they'd get the idea that I wasn't going to join the party up there.

Well, as I discovered later, that was not their intention at all. Because that September day in North Vietnam was especially hot and humid and we were at a relatively high altitude in the mountains, the air was particularly thin. "High, hot, and humid" conditions like that are the very worst kind for a helo attempting to hover, and the total weight of the helicopter then becomes an extremely critical factor. So it turned out that what the pilot was doing up over that mountain was dumping my weight of fuel, so they would be able to pick me up.

As the helo circled back along the northern ridgeline to my right in order to approach me from the valley, I heard machine guns firing at it. Later we saw that a round had hit the tail going almost vertically and its path through the tail took it upward right through the tail rotor. Had it hit the rotor, the helo would have been destroyed, most likely along with its crew.

Just then I heard one of the loudest and most beautiful sounds I'd ever experienced. The RESCAP A-1 had descended and flew over me at about 300 feet and then opened up with all four 20 mm cannons at the bad guys who were shooting at the helo. We never heard another peep from them. The helo pilots said that there was a North Vietnamese encampment about as far to the northeast from where the helo was fired upon as the helo was around the ridgeline from me. Thus, in another hour and a half or so, I would have had visitors.

The helo finally approached me and began to hover at about 40 feet above me. The crewman let down the horse collar, and I fitted it properly around me, then wrapped my arms securely around it. The crewman started to winch me up, but, instead, the helo began to settle! The thin air couldn't support a hover.

So all of a sudden the helo began to go forward to gain forward airspeed. At first I was bumping along the side of the mountain. Then, nothing but air…and lots of it.

As I dangled that forty feet below the helo, I looked up to see if I were being ratcheted up toward it. Then when I glanced down I realized that we were about five hundred feet above the valley floor; so I looked back up and chose not to look down again. After being considerably too long on the ground in enemy territory, I was finally pulled up into the helo. I nodded to the crewman and then slid as far back into the helo as humanly possible…and then began to cry like a baby. The stress had been overwhelming, and now I had a chance to be relieved of some of it.

When I could see again, I took a small Bible from my survival vest that was a going away gift from my church youth group before leaving for the Naval Academy. I turned to my favorite Psalm, the 139th, and read what I'd called my "Naval Aviator's Psalm" ever since I had run across it one night early in my Naval Academy years. Verses 7-10 (KJV) say this:

> *Whither shall I go from thy spirit?*
> *Or whither shall I flee from thy presence?*
> *If I ascend up into heaven, thou art there:*
> *If I make my bed in hell, behold, thou art there.*
> *If I take the wings of the morning,*
> *And dwell in the uttermost parts of the sea,*
> *Even there shall thy hand lead me,*
> *And thy right hand shall hold me.*

Since I had just been through all of that, dwelling in the uttermost parts of the sea (the South China Sea), then taking the wings of the morning and ascending up into heaven, and then making my bed in hell (if truly war is hell), I really felt that this helo was in many ways to me the hand of God, leading me and holding me.

But I didn't get to revel in the glory of that concept for very long, for just then the crewman's eyes grew very, very wide. Shortly he sidled over to me and said, "They're shooting at us...do you want to see?" I allowed as how I'd do just fine not seeing.

There was one particularly close blast that caused the helo to begin to vibrate. And watching between the pilots' seats I noticed that for the rest of the flight the pilot periodically kept pushing a large red button in the middle of the instrument console. For some reason I kept wondering if it were about to eject us from the helo. In any other state of mind I would have seen how ridiculous a thought that was. But right then I just kept thinking, "Oh no...not again!" (Later he told me that the close explosion had unbalanced the main rotor blades, and the red button initiated a self-balancing mechanism, which was not 100% effective, but certainly was better than nothing).

So we kind of bounced our way out to sea toward the *USS Galveston*, the cruiser from which the helo had launched. Our landing on the cruiser was uneventful, though I was to find out a year later that the ship had traveled at "flank speed" (everything it had) directly toward the North Vietnamese coast for the full two hours of the rescue just so that the helo would have a chance to reach it on its return without running out of fuel and having to ditch at sea.

I was called to the bridge after debarking the helo to meet the captain. While we were talking, he received a message that another pilot was downed, this one just off the coast of Hainan Island, the large Chinese possession in the middle of the South China Sea. We turned and steamed at flank speed again to try to pick him up, but unfortunately we arrived far too late. Some months later I heard that that downed pilot, an Air Force major by the name of Philip Smith, was the only pilot of the war to be held as a prisoner of the Communist Chinese (for seven and a half years).

After a night of remarkably sound sleep, I was once again aboard the helo, this time on the way back to the *Independence*. At a considerable distance from the carrier I noticed something very different about the flight deck. It had colors all over it...that was strange.

Earlier in the cruise I had been sitting in my aircraft preparing for a launch when two A-6 crewman who had had to eject from their plane when it was damaged, were brought aboard in a helo and had to scurry into the flight control portion of the carrier's "island," the only superstructure above the flight deck. No special ceremony welcomed them back; no one was there to greet them.

But as we approached closer to the carrier I saw what the colors on this day were. All of the squadrons of the air wing were out on deck with their separately colored baseball hats on, red and yellow for the fighters, blue (for my squadron) and orange for the attack squadrons, green for the A-6 squadron, etc. The flight deck was full of people! The admiral was there to welcome me back, the captain of the ship, as well. I was really amazed! Later I realized that the welcome back was far more than a ceremony just for me. All hands were able to bask in the achievement of recovering the first pilot of the war to be shot down inland in North Vietnam and subsequently rescued. It was good medicine for the entire ship. But, still, it was quite a homecoming for a kid from rural Louisiana.

Lt(jg) Harris greeted by the CO of the *USS Independence*,
Captain John E. Kennedy, upon his return from North Vietnam
(Official Navy Photograph)

Months later, when I had the time to review the sequence
of events during the attack, I'm pretty sure I figured out what
had happened to my aircraft. When we were circling the
reservoir prior to being called in on the target, the "different"
feeling I had about a particular movement of the aircraft was
most likely a direct hit by some type of anti-aircraft fire. It
probably entered the side of the after portion of the aircraft in
the back part of the engine, missing the critical working parts
of the engine as well as the fuel, oil and hydraulic lines. But by
penetrating in the exhaust area of the engine, super hot gases
began to escape out the side of the aircraft as well as passing
down the designed exhaust path from the back of the plane.

The plane was still flying reasonably well, although my
climb from 500 feet to 12,000 feet really may have been
slower than everyone else. By the time I had joined up with
the other A-4 and then we had caught up with the A-6, the

exhaust gases finally heated up a fire warning sensor (thus the "FIRE" warning light) and burned through the liquid oxygen line which fed 100% oxygen to my mask (that was the smell of something burning I had in my oxygen mask). But now the burning liquid oxygen had become "an acetylene torch," burning through the hydraulic line (causing the rudder pedals to "slip" and freezing the control stick). Finally the entire engine bay exploded causing the separation of the aft portion of the aircraft from the cockpit. It was a delayed shootdown.

What came from this whole adventure? First of all, a great deal of humility. Seven aircrewmen were shot down on September 20th, 1965. Six of them spent seven and a half years as POWs; only one was rescued. Those men suffered brutalization that is hard to even imagine. I'm not convinced, had I been one of them, that I would have survived the torture. I don't do pain well.

But, as well, I had rubbed shoulders with real, live, down-to-earth heroes of the grandest sort; the A-1 pilot who stayed over my downed aircraft until he was able to direct the helo to me, descending low enough to protect the helo and me by his close air support, risking his life and freedom for us; the A-4 pilots from my squadron who escorted the helo in through the anti-aircraft fire south of Haiphong by flying at a higher altitude than the helo, inviting the gunners to fire at them and therefore not noticing the helicopter; the helo pilots themselves who decided to go deep into enemy territory despite the warning that I was either dead or unconscious, and then who faced enemy retaliation at the rescue scene and on the way back to the cruiser. They also knew that there was a good chance that, even if the rescue was successful, they still might have to ditch in the sea due to a lack of fuel.

Such risks by the men involved were not personal; they were professional. Professional military personnel often risk their lives for their comrades, many times sacrificing life or limb in the process.

Throughout the cultural and societal unpopularity of the Vietnam War, I nonetheless was extremely proud to have served my country. Additionally, I was filled with great admiration for the quality and courage of the men with whom I was honored to have served.

And to top it off I learned a real lesson about *peace* in the midst of war. You see, for weeks after I was shot out of the saddle, I never smiled; I was tied up in knots emotionally. It was more than just being scared; I was able to go ahead and fly even through my fear. No, this was a deeper, soul-wrenching emotion so intense that I couldn't fully identify it…but it was very real and it was pervasive in my life.

But through prayer, the Scriptures, meditation on the character of God, and a reflection of what this life is all about in relationship to the eternal life to come, I finally reached a sense of the presence of God so profound and fundamental it has never left me. I came to realize that if I took off and was shot down and killed, I would then be with God. If I was shot down and captured, He would be with me (through whatever the enemy would throw at me). And, then, if I went out and came back with no problem, I would simply thank God, get some sleep, and do it again the next day.

Since everything after the experiences of flying in combat has been less stressful and less dangerous (save the time the pilot of the Search-and-Rescue aircraft in which I was an observer flew us into a mountain – but that's another story for another time), then I have been blessed with an inescapably firm conviction that God is there and is in control however, whenever, and wherever the spiritual battles may occur.

For you see, whenever someone has made his "bed in hell" and has survived, then he knows that "the God who is there" can give us peace wherever we may lay our head.

2.

There I Was, At 20,000 Feet Inverted, At *Night*...Really!

Surely Thou dost set them in slippery places;
Thou dost cast them down to destruction.
How they are destroyed in a moment!
They are utterly swept away by sudden terrors!
Psalm 73:18-19 NASB

When it is dark out over the ocean at night, it can be very, very dark. On a moonless night, flying under an overcast, away from all ships and any land, there simply isn't any light out there...it is inky-black dark. In fact, it can be terrifying it is so dark. The only darker place I've ever personally been in was a salt mine a thousand feet below the Louisiana surface when the lights were turned off. It was absolutely dark then...the eyes never adjusted to the light, simply because *there was NO light*!

This was the context in which I was to fly my first night combat mission after having been shot out of the saddle some four weeks before. A few days after that event the ship had left the line and had gone to Yokosuka, Japan for a couple of weeks of R & R (rest and relaxation) for the crew and the airwing.

After returning to the line, we were on a daytime schedule for the first week or so until we all got our sea legs (and combat flying wings) back. Then we were on the full midnight-to-noon or noon-to-midnight twelve-hour flight schedule. Early in that schedule I was assigned to fly an "oh-dark thirty" mission with the commanding officer of the squadron to bomb a supply encampment in southern North Vietnam. Such a mission this early in the war (October of 1965) usually did not entail a great deal of danger, even at night if one was reasonably careful, since the enemy's anti-aircraft defenses were not as extensive in the southern part of the country. Our job was simply to interdict the supplies that were flowing into South Vietnam for the Viet Cong.

However, when the squadron commander and I went to the intelligence conference room of the ship (called the *IOIC*, the "Integrated Operations and Intelligence Center"), we overheard the debrief of the pilots of a returning mission who reported surface-to-air missiles having been fired at them... and their location was *precisely where we were going*!

Uh oh! Already the throat was beginning to constrict and to get a bit drier. We had not faced SAMs since the twenty or so that were fired at our attack group during our attack on the bridge in Hanoi when I was shot down...and I'm afraid I wasn't really looking forward to seeing them again so soon!

Our mission called for the skipper to carry flares as well as bombs, and I would just have bombs. As we approached the supply encampment, he would drop some flares at about three or four thousand feet and they would slowly drift down on their parachutes, lighting up the area while we did our normal daylight bombing runs. The conventional rule about bombing to the light of flares was that you never flew under a flare, because it could be lying on the ground! Even though the flares put out an amazing amount of light, there was still the loss of most of the daytime visual cues outside the immediate area lighted by the flares. Though this type of mission was inherently dangerous due to the nature of the beast, we felt relatively secure about our ability to safely carry it out...until, of course, we heard about the surface-to-air guided missiles.

After our briefing, and when the traditional command was given to all ready rooms, "Pilots, man your aircraft," we went to the flight deck and were greeted with the blackest night you could ever hope *not* to see. Moonless and overcast at about 12,000 feet, we didn't even have the benefit of the starlight (which does provide a surprisingly sufficient amount of light on a dark night). The throat was constricting and growing drier by the minute!

Our launch and rendezvous were routine, at least as routine as it can be when one joins up on nothing more than a set of lights out in a pool of black ink. As we punched up through the overcast that was about a thousand feet thick, we arrived up on top to almost a fiery display of stars. We now had some additional visual cues, since the stars were everything "up" and they ended at the black horizon and everything that was black was "down." That was comforting, as we could now look outside our cockpits and away from out instruments and still were able to sense "wings level" and "up and down."

As we leveled out at 20,000 feet for cruising in toward our target, I slipped back to a mile behind and a thousand feet above the skipper (so that I could look "through" him at the ground and provide a second set of eyes looking for evidence of the bad guys). He turned out all of his running lights (so that those same bad guys couldn't see him) except for his upper anti-collision light, which was taped so that only the back 45 or so degrees showed. That was my only visual contact with my lead aircraft...but it was enough.

As we continued in toward the coast, we could see that some distance in front of us the overcast (now an "undercast") began to break up, and we could begin to discern the shoreline of the coast in the starlight.

The skipper began searching out the target area ahead of us, when all of a sudden it happened!

"Decoy Lead...down at eleven o'clock!!!"

What I had seen was a light, starting small and beginning to grow in intensity, followed by another doing the same thing. That was precisely the description given to us of the lifting off of the SAM 2 surface-to-air guided missiles. The fiery exhaust of the SAM would grow more intense as it approached, and the enemy always fired them one after another in pairs. The briefing we had overheard was right, and we were now facing two telephone-pole-sized missiles which were capable of hunting us down and killing us...with the emphasis on "killing us!"

"I see them," the skipper said. "Hit the deck!"

That instruction was for us to lose altitude as fast as possible in order to attempt to cause the radar which was guiding the missiles to be blocked out by a hill or confused by the ground (in this case, the sea) clutter, which would possibly interrupt the tracking capability and guidance by the radar of the missiles. And in the process we would want to put as much distance as possible between ourselves and the missiles.

The maneuver which would do everything that I wanted done right then is called the "Split S," an aerobatic maneuver in which the aircraft loses altitude, changes direction, and gains airspeed all at the same time. The pilot rolls inverted, pulls down to vertical, and, at a given time, pulls out going the opposite way from his original direction. I knew all of this, but I just had never done it at night...and only because of the *extremis* I was in would I do it now! But do it I did!

Rolling inverted, I pulled myself to a downward vertical direction. Jamming the throttle to full power, I did absolutely everything I could, including peddling, to try to get down from altitude. As I was screaming straight down, I could easily see that I was going vertically down because of the bowl of stars reaching down to the horizon all around me.

But then, at about 13,000 feet I once again plunged into the "undercast," which rapidly turned back into an overcast as I popped out the bottom of it...into absolute black-darkness. Except for the soft, red-lighted instruments telling me that I was nose-down, in a 90-degree dive, at an airspeed that I'd never approached before, passing through 12,000 feet, I could see absolutely...*nothing...else*!

That did it! That was the worst terror I had ever experienced in an aircraft! I was hurtling toward an ocean that I couldn't see at an outrageous speed for my aircraft, with a missile trying its best to catch up with me and do me in...things simply couldn't possibly get any worse...or so I thought!

As I passed through 10,000 feet, I felt that as fast as I was moving I'd better begin to pull out of my dive, so that I could round out at a couple of thousand feet above the water, heading away from the missiles. So I pulled gently back on the control stick, knowing that it wouldn't take much at that speed to begin the pullout.

THUDUDUDUDUDUDUDUD! All I got was a shudder in the aircraft while it continued plunging toward the sea! It wouldn't come out of its dive...and I had absolutely no earthly idea why. I tried again, pulling even more gently back on the stick. No luck; just a shudder and a persistent plunge toward the black sea below and inevitable destruction. I was now no more than 20 seconds from making a very small splash in a very large ocean, and I didn't have the slightest idea what was wrong or what I should do. Things had gotten ever so much worse!

Folks, at this point in the story whenever I'm telling it to an audience I usually take a break in the action to allow the audience a breather and to give me a chance to make a very emphatic point.

When Asaph, one of King David's chief musicians, wrote the 73rd Psalm, the introduction to Book III of the Psalms, he was obviously in a very conflicted frame of mind. Here are excerpts from what he says (from the NASB):

Surely God is good to Israel, to those who are pure in heart!
But as for me, my feet came close to stumbling; my steps had almost slipped.
For I was envious of the arrogant, as I saw the prosperity of the wicked.
For there are no pains in their death, and their body is fat.
They are not in trouble as other men; nor are they plagued like mankind.
Therefore pride is their necklace; the garment of violence covers them.
They mock, and wickedly speak of oppression; they speak from on high.
They have set their mouth against the heavens, and their tongue parades through the earth.
And they say, "How does God know? And is there knowledge with the Most High?"
Behold, these are the wicked; and always at ease, they have increased in wealth.

It seems to me that Asaph has surely made his case about what seems to be the constant good fortune of evil men. And I'm afraid that I have noticed similar things in our own world. The dictators of nations have palaces and power and a whole lot of possessions. They treat their people with distain and the concept of God with amused mockery. And it seems to trickle down through their minions to every petty "bad guy" in every corner of every land on earth. The rats always seem to be winning the rat race.

And then Asaph goes on to lament his own status in life. See if this doesn't sound familiar:

Surely in vain I have kept my heart pure, and washed my

hands in innocence;
For I have been stricken all day long, and chastened every
morning.

Whoa! Doesn't he speak for most of those of us who live
in the real world, especially during the down periods of life
when it seems as if nothing is going right and the promise
of our faith seems to turn to ashes? Undoubtedly Asaph was
having a particularly bad day when he wrote this…but he
then made a discovery that should challenge us all.

If I had said, "I will speak thus," behold, I should have
betrayed the generation of Thy children. When I pondered to
understand this, it was troublesome in my sight until I came
into the sanctuary of God; then I perceived their end.

"Then I perceived their end!" That's it! When we are
in "sanctuary" with God, when He is able to break through
the clutter of the worries and cares of our world and speak
directly Spirit to spirit, we discover the sad state of the few
years of victory the "wicked" may have in this world, and
how it contrasts with "their end," their eternal destiny. Here's
what Asaph has to say about that:

Surely Thou dost set them in slippery places; Thou dost cast
them down to destruction.
How they are destroyed in a moment! They are utterly swept
away by sudden terrors!

Oh my…I can't even read that without feeling an unmiti-
gated sadness of heart mixed with my own sense of horror.
Because, you see, it was that same terror I was experiencing
that night off the coast of North Vietnam. Most of those who
are "the wicked" see themselves above others, above the law,
and perhaps even above God. In reality, however, in much
of their lives they are simply trying to escape that which is
pursuing them and which ultimately will destroy them, the

reality of their own mortality and their inability to overcome it. And the more they try to escape that destruction, the more they are rushing to a destruction of their own making…as I was that night.

Let me explain as I continue the narrative. After the second attempt to pull the aircraft out of its dive, I did something inexplicable, to a degree nonsensical, and with absolutely no purpose whatsoever…I reduced my power, pulling the throttle back to its "Idle" setting. A rational thought would have told me that wouldn't help to delay my rush to destruction a millisecond; it wouldn't give me any more time to contemplate my predicament, nor would it cushion the impending collision with an unforgiving South China Sea.

But something told me to reduce my power, and so I did. And then I pulled ever so gently on the stick, and the aircraft began to respond! I had no idea why it did now and why it hadn't a couple of seconds before…but right then, "mine was not to reason why," mine was only to attempt to complete the pullout before the plane hit the water. It was now a battle of aerodynamics versus gravity and momentum.

Holding my breath and seeking divine intervention, I tenuously played the amount of pull on the stick in order to level the aircraft out against the potential for pulling too hard and jerking the plane into a stall, followed by "spin, crash, burn and die." All too slowly my descent began to slow and my nose attitude began to rise toward the horizon…3000 feet, 2500, 2000, 1500, 1200, 1000…and finally level at 800 feet!

I was alive, the plane was flying normally, and no SAMs had found their way up my tailpipe…wow! After a couple of minutes of regrouping to insure that I was going to be able to complete the flight, I contacted the skipper. We discussed a rendezvous point, joined up, continued to an alternate target, and returned to the carrier for the easiest part of this particular flight, a night carrier landing. With what had just occurred, a night carrier landing was going to be a piece of cake!

It took months for me to figure out what likely had happened during that minute or so of pure terror. Here's how I see it:

When the skipper and I saw the lift-off of the SAMs, we were very early in the flight, thus we had most of our fuel and all of our bombs. Since I carried six five-hundred-pound general-purpose bombs (500 lb. GP bombs), that 3000 pounds plus approximately 9000 lbs of fuel meant that I was flying a very heavy aircraft. So, when I rolled inverted and pulled through to the vertical and went to full power, I quickly accelerated to a blazing speed for the A4, a decidedly *sub*sonic aircraft. The A4 was not built to go *super*-sonic; therefore going supersonic would have had disastrous consequences for my subsonic bird.

However, as it was, I reached the speed of sound as I was screaming down from 20,000 feet. That meant I was going at about 700 mph! As I approached Mach 1, my plane went *tran*sonic, meaning that the compressed-air wave (generally called the "sonic boom") was playing over my control surfaces, disrupting the airflow and their ability to control the aircraft. That's why it only shuddered when I pulled back on the stick.

It was then that the magical or miraculous or, as I've come to believe, the Spirit-guided decision to pull back on my throttle (when nothing else worked) decreased my speed almost imperceptibly, but just sufficiently to get me out of transonic flight where the airflow over my control surfaces again became normal, allowing me to pull out of the fastest dive I was ever in as a pilot.

And here's the kicker…I was trying to evade that which was pursuing me and attempting to destroy me. In doing so, I placed myself in a destructive mode without knowing it, and the more the power I utilized in my frenzied attempt to escape, the more certain was my approaching destruction.

It was not until I was willing to yield up my power (of

propulsion) to allow a higher power (of aerodynamics) to come into play that I was able to escape the coming destruction. Not until I slowed sufficiently to allow the control surfaces of the aircraft to once again take control, could I then fly the aircraft out of harm's way.

And, of course, there is a very unsubtle analogy to be made here for those in our personal worlds who are spiritually in that terrifying situation in which I was physically that dark night in October of 1965. Many with whom we come in contact are lost in the black darkness of sin. They're scared, they're running from the Destroyer, and they're using whatever power they have to escape...only they're simply rushing headlong into eternal destruction.

But we have good news for them. There is a way of escape, a way to life and peace. But they must do the hardest thing possible for them; they must give up their own power, their own power to control their lives, to control their relationships, to control their environment. They've simply got to yield control over to that Higher Power which can bring them to safety.

Spiritually they must accept that the power of God through a personal relationship with Jesus Christ, God the Son, is more than able to protect them from the destruction behind them and before them. That power is sufficient to forgive sins, to change lives, and to give them eternal life in the presence of The Almighty.

When that happens in a person's life, then, just as in that night back there in my past, coming aboard God's eternal "carrier" at the end of our life's final "flight," no matter how rough the sea and how howling the winds, it truly will be "a piece of cake."

Amen and amen!

3.

THINGS THAT GO
"WHOOSH" IN THE NIGHT…
AND SOMETIMES DURING THE DAY, TOO

You will not be afraid of the terror by night,
Or of the arrow that flies by day.
Psalm 91:5 NASB

He was very wise, this Naval Academy aerodynamics professor of mine.

"Anyone who flies high-performance jet aircraft is going to experience many 'near misses' during his career," he concluded one day. He had just recounted for us the time he watched a jet that, attempting to land on the carrier, overshot the arresting wires, continued off the angled deck, and then disappeared below the flight deck, only to reappear several seconds later barely wallowing above the waves, struggling to stay airborne and to gain airspeed. I never forgot that axiomatic statement, for circumstance brought it often back to mind.

And not every time were those circumstances self-inflicted. When I was placed in harm's way by choice of profession or even by my own carelessness or mistakes, that was one thing. At least I couldn't blame others for *those* 'near misses'. But when I was jeopardized by someone else's failures or incompetence, then it seemed as though the circumstances themselves were ganging up on me to try their best to do me in.

For example, my first aviation 'near miss' happened even before I got out of high school. My retired-navy-chief dad was finally getting his college degree (having entered the navy at 17 and then having retired at 37). He had wanted to teach school early on and was now preparing himself to do so. This particular summer between my freshman and sophomore years of high school he was out of town at a different college picking up some credits that he couldn't get at our local college.

My mom, my brother, and I had decided to go to the drive-in movie one evening and were just getting in our car parked in the garage. Just then we began to hear the strangest, persisting "whoosh" we'd ever heard, growing louder and louder. It just didn't register in any of us as to what could be making that sound, as we glanced at each other in increasing concern.

Then there was a mighty explosion! I peeked around the side of the garage and saw flames leaping high above the trees just a block or so away!

"It crashed!!!," I shouted, as I took off at full speed toward the fire. Sure enough, exactly two blocks away, right next to the small National Cemetery in our town, precisely in *that* block where *our* garage was located in *our* block, there was a huge crater with what looked like a pancaked automobile smoking in the middle of it.

The house next to the crater was on fire, so I asked the man standing there whether anyone was in the house. He answered that he didn't think so...but he seemed rather confused and out of it. He told me that he had been asleep in a second-story bedroom of the house when the plane hit the garage next to the house. So he had to jump out of a window to escape the flames and had sprained his ankle. His ankle injury and a small cut on the hand of a fireman when the fire brigade arrived were the only injuries of the whole event.

We found out later that a jet fighter from the near-by England Air Force Base had flamed out approaching the airfield for landing, and the pilot had ejected. He parachuted safely into the local college football stadium. The aircraft had then rolled inverted, proceeded over our house and then nosed down into the garage two blocks away. The unearthly sound we heard was the aircraft speeding toward and over us with its engine off. For months after that experience whenever any of the three of us heard a low-flying aircraft, we would cringe, duck, sigh heavily, and then smile sheepishly at one another. That first aviation 'near miss' had come literally too close to home!

The next time I would combine a "whoosh" with a 'near miss' was some nine years later and precisely two weeks before I was shot down in North Vietnam. Our carrier had been "on the line" for our second line period since the last week of August 1965. Most of our targets thus far had been just like our first line period, "Rolling Thunder" missions into North Vietnam. But for a few days starting about the first of September we were being diverted to some targets in South Vietnam for close air support of our troops and attacks on Viet Cong positions and supply efforts.

Our target of the evening of September 6th was an "In-country target," designating it a Forward Air Controlled (FAC) target over South Vietnam. On this particular night the target was a Viet Cong rest camp that the airborne forward air controller had just found. His calls had amassed a goodly armada of aircraft. Besides our three, there were four other four-plane divisions, both Navy and Air Force.

It was one of those very dark nights because it was moonless and there was an overcast. But, because we were in South Vietnam, we had little concern over anti-aircraft fire, guided missiles, or enemy aircraft. All we had to do was to insure we didn't get tangled up with any of our own planes.

To that end, the FAC gave us all very clear directions. He said he would fire a rocket flare into the camp. The F-4's, which were the first at the target and which had flares for night bombing, were to be first in, dropping their flares at three to four thousand feet. The flares, which provided an immense amount of light (about a million candlepower), floated slowly down on parachutes. While they were aloft and alight, we could do our bombing runs as though it were daytime...since the target area was so well lighted. The F-4's were to circle around after dropping their flares and then fire their pods of rockets into the target area. The F-4's were all armed with LAU-3's, launching pods that carried nineteen 2.75-inch rockets apiece. The rockets were unguided, so they formed a serious dispersal pattern as they approached the ground. Originally designed during WWII for fighters to fire at heavy bombers, they were extremely effective for widely-dispersed ground targets as well. After firing their rockets, the F-4's were to depart and each of the other divisions would then make runs and fire their rockets or drop their bombs.

Besides directing the order of activity over the target, the FAC also gave us a run-in heading and a departure heading so that everyone would know the flow of traffic. All the FAC had to do after giving his directions was to fire his flare into the camp and then circle in an area that would keep him out of harm's way while he fine-tuned the action, if necessary, by radio.

As the first division of F-4's completed their two runs and departed, the division of which I was the third aircraft was informed that we would follow the next set of F-4's onto the target. My division leader slowly descended from our holding altitude to our run-in altitude so that we'd be ready to make our run as soon as the fighters ahead of us had departed the pattern.

And then it was our turn. The two aircraft ahead of me peeled off in order and started their dive. I delayed until they were clear and began my run. The flares were still lighting the area, so the run was very much a textbook 45-degree bombing run. I sighted the burning flare in the trees originally fired by the FAC and pickled my bombs on it.

As I began my pullout, I turned as I climbed out so that I'd be departing out the bearing that the FAC had given. I settled on the bearing and continued my climb to altitude.

But then I saw something that I couldn't quite make out. It seemed to be a set of lights up ahead…and the lights looked like they were coming down toward me. But that couldn't be; I checked my bearing, and, just as I thought, I was precisely on the *departure* heading. But it was apparent that some fool was in a firing run coming right down the opposite of the departure heading. What was he thinking?! Obviously he was thinking that he was on the run-in heading!! And he was heading directly for me!

Just when I thought it couldn't get any worse, I'm afraid it did. At least I was able to discern that it was one of the F-4's, because right at that moment the jerk fired a pod of 19 wildly gyrating 2.75-inch rockets, any one of which could take out my A-4 in a flash, and they were all heading directly toward me!

Having an aviator's natural aversion to making abrupt and extreme flight maneuvers at night and relatively close to the ground, nevertheless I saw that this was one of those situations that called for the most abrupt and extreme measures possible! Reflexively I pulled the aircraft hard to the right and down, since it seemed that the rockets were coming toward my upper left quadrant. I held the diving turn for two or three seconds, leveled out, and kept flying away from the departure bearing. After a few more seconds I rolled back to the left to ensure that I had cleared the pattern of the rockets. Sure enough, they had barely missed me and were now nearing the ground. And I could have sworn that I heard the "whoosh" as they passed.

As I recovered my aircraft and my composure, I radioed to the assembled planes, "All aircraft...be aware that someone is flying in-bound on the departure bearing and firing rockets in the process!" I was hoping to remain professional in my communication while still letting some "plumber" (a naval aviation term for a sub-standard pilot) know that he almost shot me out of the sky.

I wish I could say that that was my last "whoosh/near miss" combination. But there was one more that had some very interesting residual effects.

This last "whooshy near miss" occurred a month after my shootdown and just about three weeks before we were to leave the line for home on November 11th, ironically enough, Veteran's Day 1965. And to be perfectly honest it was nobody's fault really...it simply happened, since I was doing the job I had to do because I had chosen the profession that required it. But later, when recounting this particular event to a special gathering back home in the States, I experienced a very moving and meaningful reaction.

This happened to be a daylight mission in which I was once again flying as the wingman for the skipper of my squadron. As the junior pilot in the squadron, I was paired with him on about a third of my nearly one hundred combat missions. This time weather precluded our going on our primary mission in North Vietnam, one that required us to scour a designated area for surface-to-air missile sites and to attack them if possible.

Instead, we had to revert to our secondary mission, to attack a bridge south of the city of Thanh Hoa. This bridge, like so many by this time even this early in the war, was a temporary replacement for a more permanent structure we had already destroyed. It was a rickety-looking wooden structure, which still did the job of allowing supply trucks to cross the river, and had the added bonus of being easily repaired no matter how many times we blew it up. Nevertheless, we were supposed to blow it up that day, at least to slow down the supply lines.

The entire attack group consisted of an A-6 Intruder (the only aircraft among us at that time that had anti-missile electronics available), two A-4's from our sister squadron, and the CO and me. The A-6 driver found the bridge pretty easily with the navigation by his B/N (bombardier/navigator) and was the first to attack. Each aircraft in our attack group was armed with Snakeyes (Mark 82 {500 lb. low-drag} bombs with retarding-fin assemblies). These bombs allowed for a low-and-slow bombing run that provided much greater accuracy, because, with the retarding-fins that would deploy when the bombs were dropped, the bombs would slow greatly, allowing the aircraft to escape the bomb explosion and fragmentation. On this particular mission, however, the low-and-slow run was one of the most harrowing of my combat career.

Each of us made our run directly down the length of the bridge so that we would hit somewhere on the bridge, even if we were short or long of our aiming point, as long as we were on line of the bridge. But that raised the major problem of this mission. You see, there were anti-aircraft guns at both ends of the bridge. The 37-millimeter guns were rapid fire, highly accurate guns, perfect for just this type of defense. Firing up to 180 rounds a minute, these guns could lay down a blanket of anti-aircraft fire that was difficult to penetrate.

So that was what each plane and each pilot was faced with on this dank and gloomy October day in North Vietnam. The A-6 made his bombing run first, dropping his entire load of 18 Snakeyes. The skipper and I followed in turn. When I rolled in, lined up on the bridge, and began the shallow and relatively slow dive on the center of the bridge, I began to pick up something in my peripheral vision as I focused on the bombsight on the top center of my instrument console. That "something" happened to be streaks that were whizzing past my canopy at a rate of one every couple of seconds or so.

Those "streaks" were obviously "tracers," specially made

rounds for the anti-aircraft guns that produced a luminescent trail allowing the gunner to visually track the flight of his shots. This was an invaluable tool for helping him to aim at the target. All that was rattling around in my head with a couple of other disturbing facts about tracers.

First of all, tracer rounds were generally placed at intervals of from one every ten rounds to one every twenty rounds. Since I was seeing one every couple or three seconds, that meant that there were at least nine other rounds whizzing past me during each two or three-second interval that I couldn't see. That gave me no comfort at all!

Secondly, I had heard that, were you to see a tracer start to glow, seemingly to simply remain in place, and then suddenly explode past your windscreen, you happened to be flying directly down the barrel of the anti-aircraft gun! And that is precisely what every one of these tracers was doing...lighting up, not perceptively moving, but just getting brighter, and then "whooshing" past my canopy in an obviously rapid series of very-near misses. The bad guys had me in their sights, and if I was going to drop my bombs on target, I was simply going to have to continue down the barrel of that gun.

It was perhaps the most nerve-wracking 15-20 seconds of flying I ever forced myself to endure...holding steady, on line, on dive-angle, on airspeed until I reached the proper altitude to release my bombs, knowing that at any second I could and, in reality, should be hit. Finally I arrived at the release altitude and pickled my bombs. As soon as I was certain they had released, I pulled hard up and to the right and began a wild series of rapid turns and abrupt altitude changes all at full power (a technique called "jinking" or "jinxing") to preclude the gunners from having a chance of locking on and hitting me before I was out of range.

But as soon as I was out of the dive and jinking my way out of range, something began to tweak at my mind...I had seen no explosions at all from any of the bombs any of the aircraft had dropped. So I pulled hard around so that I could see the bridge at about the time my bombs should have exploded, and there was nothing but silence and tranquility. The bombs had failed to go off! I had just put my life on the line for a bunch of duds, as had each of the other pilots. We were not happy campers at all! We may have damaged or destroyed the bridge, but it was only by the sheer weight of the iron bombs that fell on it.

When we got back to the carrier, we figured out what probably had happened.

The Mark 82 Snakeyes were designed to arm in two steps to protect the pilot and his aircraft. When the bomb was released, a wire firmly attached to the MBR (multiple bomb rack) on the aircraft was pulled out of the bomb causing the retarding fins of the bomb to open in the air stream. When the fins opened, a wire attached to the retarding fins mechanism was pulled out of the fuse in the nose, enabling it to arm. The reason the fuse wouldn't arm until the fins opened is that, if the fins didn't open, the low-drag configuration of the bomb with the fins closed would have allowed the bomb to travel right along with and under the aircraft until the bomb's impact. And, since the aircraft was going low, as well as slow, if the bomb were armed, the explosion and fragmentation would happen right below the aircraft and would likely cause damage or destruction of the aircraft. However, with the fins open, the bomb would fall well behind the aircraft before it impacted and exploded.

So, obviously one of two things had occurred. Either the wire attached to the MBR in every one of the bombs inadvertently separated from the aircraft not allowing the fins to open, or the fins either malfunctioned themselves (which is more likely) or the wire to the fuse didn't pull out, preventing the arming of the bomb.

Whatever the cause, not one of the forty-two bombs on the aircraft from three different squadrons functioned properly, which indicated a systems failure in the bombs rather than human failure in the armament personnel of the squadrons.

That fact came into play several years later. I was visiting my brother, who was, at the time, commanding a naval reserve outfit in Raleigh, NC. He invited me to attend a meeting of the unit and to tell them of some of my wartime experiences. In response to a question as to my most intense experience (and due to a time limit not allowing a full recitation of some of my other adventures), I chose to relate this incident. The men listened intently and were fully engaged in the action and emotion of the episode.

Though all the members of the unit were very attentive, I noticed one man in particular who seemed to be struggling greatly with the story. At the end of my talk, and when the men were dismissed, this particular individual made his way up to me, almost in tears.

He said, "Sir, I want to apologize to you."

I was caught somewhat off guard. "I'm sorry...I don't understand."

He went on, "Back in the early sixties, I worked at a plant that produced the retarding-fin components for the Mark 82 Snakeye bombs. I feel that I am personally responsible for what happened to you back then, and I want to apologize to you as a representative for those of us whose mistakes caused those bombs to malfunction and for you to have risked your life without being able to complete your mission. I truly am sorry."

Seeing how emotional and terrifically sincere he was, I was moved by his concern and his actions. I took the hand he offered in both of mine and replied as earnestly as I could, "You can't know how much I appreciate your willingness to step up and to acknowledge a manufacturing failure that was nearly so costly to us that day. I doubt that you personally were involved in those particular bombs, but I understand and am moved by your concern. I accept your apology for all of us who were affected that day and by any subsequent results of the mistakes made until they were recognized and corrected. It is so meaningful to know that those in the production and supply chain do care what happens at the action end of the line. Thank you."

And so we parted, each having experienced a new realization of an interrelated camaraderie in each individual's small but critical cog in the national machinery of the defense of liberty and protection and projection of freedom…at least in the best of all worlds.

But, of course, we don't live in the best of all worlds. Ever since Adam and Eve decided that they needed to gain their knowledge and power from the apple instead of from God, this has been a far cry from "the best of all worlds." In our world there is pain and fear and turmoil and confusion and sickness and injury and death. And throughout everything, most spend their time, energy, substance, and emotions in just trying to evade all of the above.

And yet, the things that go "bump" or "whoosh" in the night are ever-present. They are there; they sneak up and grab us and try their best to rob us of our peace and serenity and contentment. And we simply need to know where to go for protection from life's 'near misses' and things that go 'whoosh' in the night.

The Bible once again has the answer. In one of the most beautiful chapters of promises in the entire Word of God, the 91st Psalm gives God's promise of:

"The Security of the One Who Trusts in the LORD"

He who dwells in the shelter of the Most High will abide in the shadow of the Almighty. I will say to the LORD, "My refuge and my fortress, my God, in whom I trust!" For it is He who delivers you from the snare of the trapper, and from the deadly pestilence. He will cover you with His pinions, and under His wings you may seek refuge; His faithfulness is a shield and bulwark.

You will not be afraid of the terror by night, or of the arrow that flies by day; of the pestilence that stalks in darkness, or of the destruction that lays waste at noon. A thousand may fall at your side, and ten thousand at your right hand; but it shall not approach you. For you have made the LORD, my refuge, even the Most High, your dwelling place. No evil will befall you, nor will any plague come near your tent. For He will give His angels charge concerning you, to guard you in all your ways.

"Because he has loved Me, therefore I will deliver him; I will set him securely on high, because he has known My name. He will call upon Me, and I will answer him;

I will be with him in trouble; I will rescue him, and honor him. With a long life I will satisfy him, and let him behold My Salvation."

Psalm 91:1-7, 9-11, 14-16 NASB

Amen!

4.

CLOSE CALLS

You intended to harm me, but God intended
it for good to accomplish what is now being done,
the saving of many lives.
Genesis 50:20 NIV

"**D**ecoy Three Zero Four…Point Five…Ball."
That cryptic report was my "in the groove" radio
call to the LSO and to the world, at least to the world of the
USS Independence and her aircraft-recovery team that early-
November afternoon in 1965, as she was steaming around in
the South China Sea.

"Decoy"…that was the call sign of my squadron, VA-72,
Aviation Attack Squadron Seventy-Two.

"Three Zero Four"…that was the plane's side number,
304, and that identified me as the pilot who was about to land
to Pri-Fly (Primary Flight Control) and the "Air Boss," who
was in overall charge of launching and recovering all aircraft.

"Point Five"…Whoa!! What?! I'll cover that in a minute!

"Ball"…that meant I had visually acquired the "meatball" on the Fresnel Lens Landing System and was prepared
to land the aircraft.

But what was this "Point Five?"! In that portion of the "Ball call," I was supposed to be reporting the amount of fuel I had aboard my aircraft. The arresting-wire technicians used that figure plus the empty weight of the basic aircraft to set the proper amount of pressure in the hydraulic cylinders below deck to which the arresting wires were attached. But that call by all accounts should have been in the range of "Two point Oh" to "Three Point Oh," signifying that I had from 2.0 thousand pounds to 3.0 thousand pounds of fuel remaining in my aircraft.

The type aircraft I flew during this combat cruise was the A-4E Skyhawk. The "Scooter," as it was affectionately known because of its diminutive size, usually began a mission with 9,400 pounds of fuel, roughly 1,375 gallons. Fifty-four hundred pounds (775 gallons) of the kerosene-like JP-5 fuel was carried in the internal wing and fuselage tanks, and the remaining 4,000 pounds was in two 300-gallon (2,000-pound) under-wing drop tanks. A normal two-hour flight would use up about 75% of the available fuel. But, then again, who said we were flying "normal" flights out here?

"Point Five" indicated that I had .5 thousand pounds of fuel; 500 pounds!! First of all, the fuel indicator was simply not that accurate. I might be running on fumes. Even if I really *had* five hundred pounds, that was not likely going to get me all the way around again if I didn't get aboard on this first try.

In my entire aviation career I was only this low on fuel *while still in the air* on one other occasion. That's when I pulled a stupid on a cross county flight while I was in a "proficiency flight status" (requiring only eight flight hours a month) as a company officer at the Naval Academy. During that flight from Andrews AFB in Washington D. C. to Dobbins AFB just northwest of Atlanta, Georgia, I had planned on an "en route descent," stretching my fuel availability to the max. What I hadn't planned on was a change in the jet stream in both direction and altitude.

The route from Andrews to Dobbins was directly south-west. The jet stream flows generally from west to east and usually only affects in a major way flight in the 30,000 to 40,000-foot range. On this particular venture though, the air masses forming the jet stream were out to get me. They positioned themselves such that the jet stream dipped sharply down out of the Rockies all the way to the Gulf of Mexico through central Texas and then abruptly swung northeast through Georgia right up to Maryland. Northeast is directly opposite of southwest.

Uh oh! And besides that, the level of the jet stream dropped amazingly low, so that at 25,000 feet in my T-1 jet, I was facing a head wind that had not been predicted of almost 120 knots, and as I began my en route let-down, even passing through 15,000 I was fighting nearly a 100-knot head wind. That meant that my 170-knot "idle descent" (the throttle was set at "idle," which was 70% of full power) was only covering 70 knots over the ground (which was roughly 90 mph). Some of the "aggressive drivers" on the highway below me were going as fast as I was!

That also meant that I was coming down well short of my destination and had to make up the distance at low altitude, which burned a whole lot more fuel than at higher altitude. As I had long-since passed my divert base, I was committed to continuing on to Dobbins. But it was anyone's guess whether I would have the gas to make it.

As I approached the airfield at about five miles out, I called the tower to request an immediate landing. The controller told me that I was "number two" for landing behind a huge transport plane that I could barely make out miles and miles away on an extended approach. At that point, I'm afraid I had to go to confession.

"Look, Dobbins Tower…I'm a small jet that is just about at the end of the runway. I'm short on fuel, and in no way at all can I wait to land behind your transport. I promise you I can sneak in before him, land, and get off the runway before he's even close. But, if you insist on my following him, I'll just have to declare an emergency and ruin both of our days."

"Uh, Roger, Navy Jet...you're number one for landing."

"Roger, I'm number one. Thank you very much, Tower."

I landed with 200 pounds of fuel remaining and was very surprised I didn't flame out taxiing to my parking spot!

But that was then, and this was now. Let me tell you how I got into *this* pickle, and why landing with barely enough fuel left to get aboard the carrier was still the least stressful part of the latter portion of this flight.

Each pilot aboard the *Independence* was acutely aware that we were less than a week from leaving the line and going home. If a pilot could survive the next six days, he would be "home free" in its most literal sense. So every "relatively safe" flight was like money in the bank. And that November day I was scheduled for just about the safest combat flight we normally had available, a RESCAP mission.

RESCAP stands for REScue Combat Air Patrol. It signified that the aircraft involved would be flying off the coast of North Vietnam, available first for protecting the SAR (Search and Rescue) ships—usually destroyers—and the on-station HU-16 Albatross, an amphibious aircraft, which was capable of landing at sea to pick up downed airmen. But, as well, the RESCAP aircraft could be diverted over land to assist in the SAR effort for a downed pilot or aircrew in Bad-Guys-Land.

But, usually those hops got very boring, flying large circles above and around the Albatross (if we could link up with him) or simply being in the area and in contact in the event some untoward action should take place in relationship to the Albatross, the destroyer, or aircraft over land. In fact, generally the highlight of the mission was when the destroyer would ask for a high-speed pass. At that we'd give a loud "Whoopee!" and dive down from altitude gaining a whole bunch of airspeed and skimming so close to the water we'd kick up "rooster tails." Then we'd buzz the destroyer close enough to knock the captain's coffee cup out of his hand. We never failed to get a BZ ("Bravo Zulu" – flag and Morse Code communications for "Well Done!") from the destroyer's crew.

On this mission I was paired with the same pilot that I joined up with after the attack on Hanoi and who tried his best to get me out of my burning plane by shouting over the radio, "I've got you...YOU'RE ON FIRE!! YOU'RE ON FIRE!! EJECT!!! EJECT!!!" I heard the "I've got you," but I was already traveling up the rails in my ejection seat when he saw the explosion. Again, since he was senior to me even though he was in VA-72's sister A-4 squadron, he led the hop and I was his wingman.

Although our ship's attack-*de-jour* was cancelled that day, our presence as RESCAPers was necessary because there was an ongoing SAR mission for a downed air force pilot about sixty miles inland in North Vietnam. His position was just above the 20th parallel, where the coastline makes a 90-degree jog to the east about 20 miles or so north of Thanh Hoa (pronounced "Than Wah," and, yes, this does come into play later).

However, we weren't called in to assist with the SAR activities when we got on station orbiting the SAR destroyer. It appeared that we were simply going to have another ho-hummer, unless, of course, "somebody down there" wanted a high-speed pass. But, we got no call from anyone, so when we reached our bingo fuel state, we turned and headed toward the carrier.

Not so fast! Just *then* we got a call to join the search effort over the karst ridges (razor-sharp-looking ridges poking almost vertically up out of some of the Vietnam plains) where the pilot was thought to have gone down. Oooo-kay.

Low fuel and all, here we come.

As we coasted in over the east-west delta, Gary whistled over his radio and asked, "Did you see *that*?!"

"Negative...what was it?"

"It was a SAM site with three missiles on their launchers!"

"Gulp!!"

We continued on our way at about 8,000 feet (just above the altitude limit of the more prevalent 37 mm ack-ack guns), until we found the area where the pilot was supposed to have ejected. We began to search the area while circling at 8K, so I stepped up about five hundred feet and slid to the outside of Gary's circle. That was so that I could look "through" him at the ground, all the while keeping him in sight and checking for stray bad guys trying to get him (that's called "protecting his six").

We made several circles in silence, until I realized *it shouldn't have been in silence.* I called Gary and got no answer. Uh oh, again. I had a bad radio. I reached down to fiddle with the connections from my oxygen mask (transmitter) and helmet (receivers) to the radio panel to see if that would help. When I looked up, Gary was gone!

Just then I came out from behind a puffy little cloud and found him again. (Back at the carrier later Gary told me that, when I disappeared, he called me and got no response and was sure that I had gotten myself shot down again!)

But that wasn't our problem just at this moment. Our problem was that when I visually reacquired Gary, he was being followed...by large puffs of black smoke! Every two or three seconds a new puff would appear, slowly walking right up behind him. It was obviously a 55-millimeter radar-controlled anti-aircraft gun that had locked onto him and was about to get him.

Trusting that my radio was now operational, I only had time to yell his squadron call sign and tell him to break away,

"Sidewinder…BREAK RIGHT…*NOW!!*"

Without hesitation, any of which would have been fatal, he broke sharply to the right on my command, and the next puff was precisely where he would have been had he continued in his direction. I had finally gotten to return the favor to Gary for being there for me when I was in trouble.

But Gary's present problems were not over…not by a long shot (no pun intended). The gunner was doing his best to lock onto him again, and black puffs were all around him. By the way, those black "puffs" were not just smoke… they were fragments of the AA shell that could tear up an airplane's wing or tail or engine, or could take the pilot out by hitting near the cockpit.

Gary shouted for me to head back to the ship! He then jettisoned his empty drop tanks so that he could maneuver better, rolled over into a vertical dive, and did his best to pull a disappearing act as he attempted make his way back to the carrier.

Actually I was not really in danger at this point, because all the attention was directed at him. So, I checked my TACAN bearing to the ship, went to full power, and began a climb. I realized that I was already seriously low on fuel and needed to preserve all I could in the hundred-or-so-mile trip back to the carrier.

Recognizing just how close it was going to be, I radioed approach control that I had to have an en route, "idle descent" (how ironic) to a "straight in" approach…I couldn't afford any twists and turns. They gave me precisely what I needed. The ship was turned into the wind, everyone was in place, and all I had to do was to get aboard.

As I said, that was the least stressful part of the latter portion of this hop, because landing aboard the carrier was one of my better skills as a naval aviator. I was generally near the top in the graded competition of landing average in our squadron. So, excepting a hook-skip (where the hook bounces over the wire—uncommon but not entirely rare) or some other very out-of-the-ordinary happening, I was pretty certain I would be able to get safely down. And I did.

But I didn't see Gary's plane on board right then.

Later, when he finally made it back, he got together with me for a debrief, and he sheepishly told me what had happened after he escaped the initial barrage of anti-aircraft fire. When he had dropped his fuel tanks and dived toward the ground, he leveled off at about 3,000 feet, hoping he could get by the gunners simply by flying so fast at the lower altitude he would be past them before they could train their guns on him.

It was not a bad idea…except for one minor detail. Our bearing back to the ship was about 135 degrees, to the southeast paralleling the long central and southern North Vietnam and the northern South Vietnam coastlines. But up where we were searching and where all the fireworks were, the coastline ran almost directly south.

That was one fact that had escaped Gary in the confusion and stress of trying to keep from getting blasted out of the sky like a clay pigeon. So, when he leveled out at 3,000 feet, he paralleled the coast all right, but he was heading directly south. And at that point he was directly north of Thanh Hoa, one of the largest and most heavily defended cities in North Vietnam. And my friend, Gary, had decided to fly right down Main Street at 3,000 feet. I really don't have any idea how we got him back…and frankly, neither did he.

Fortunately there is one thing that is invariably true about leading a flight that saved Gary. Since all the wingmen must use additional fuel in staying in position on the leader, the flight leader has more fuel remaining for landing than the wingmen, or in this case, the wing*man*. And, as well, Gary's plane had a clean wing, since he had dropped the two drop-tanks. So, though he had the same distance back to the ship as I did, and he was flying a goodly portion of it at 3,000 feet having to dodge all sorts of anti-aircraft fire, yet, when he found he was still alive south of the city, he was able to get to the coast, climb to altitude, and shoot a straight-in approach, landing with just about, you guessed it, 500 lbs. of fuel.

It was obvious that we had literally dodged a bullet in the midst of a whole passel of close calls; the SAM site with missiles at the ready, the separation by the cloud when my radio was on the blink that could have allowed either of us to have been picked off without the other one really knowing what had happened, the extremely fortuitous timing of getting my radio back and spotting Gary again just at the time calamity was about to march right up his tailpipe, his escaping the barrage of AA blasts at altitude and then somehow making it through the gauntlet of Thanh Hoa's anti-aircraft defenses like a salmon making it upstream with a "herd" of grizzlies in the river, and finally each of us having just enough petrol in the tank to get us home safely for a shower, sprucing up, and then dinner in the wardroom at 1800 hours. A-mazing!

Later when I began recounting the close calls just in this hop, I was reminded of the story of Joseph in the Old Testament and the number of close calls he endured before God had accomplished His will through him of preparing a land for the birth of a nation, the birth of the Jewish Nation. (Genesis 37-50)

First of all, Joseph was dearly hated by is ten older brothers. He was so obviously his father's favorite, since he was the first-born son by his father's favorite wife, Rachel, and, as well, he had this irritating air about him that he was better than they and that ultimately they would, at some point of their lives, bow down to him.

Secondly, when he visited them on one occasion while they were tending the sheep, they determined to kill him and tell their father that a wild animal had done so. Only a petition of the eldest brother for mercy protected his life.

So rather than kill him, they sold him to a merchant train

going to Egypt. There he was sold as a slave to the captain of Pharaoh's guard, a very important man, indeed. Potiphar, this very important man, soon saw the great potential in Joseph and ultimately placed him in charge of the administration of his entire household, because, as the Scripture tells us, the LORD was with Joseph.

Potiphar's wife also saw a great deal of potential in Joseph, but not for the best of reasons…and, as we all know, "Hell hath no fury like a woman scorned." Indeed Potiphar's wife was a woman scorned…by a man of integrity. So naturally she lied to her husband about Joseph, and hubby immediately tossed him into the lock-up. Undoubtedly Potiphar could have had Joseph put to death—slaves were a cheap commodity in those days. But, something caused him only to imprison his chief steward.

Then it was the keeper of the keys who also saw the great potential in Joseph, because the LORD was with him. So, in time the prison warden put Joseph in charge of everything and everybody in the prison.

Finally, after being ignored and forgotten for years by those he had helped while they were in the prison, Joseph was called before Pharaoh to interpret some dreams he had experienced that confused and frightened him. Joseph told Pharaoh that *he* could not interpret the dreams but that *God* would give him the answers. And when He did, Pharaoh saw the great potential in Joseph and placed him in charge of the *entire kingdom*, to protect it from the coming famine.

And we know that was when his brothers *did* bow down before him, without realizing who he was. When they found out, they were at once delighted and frightened, assuming that Joseph likely would take revenge on them.

But, of course, Joseph could see the hand of God in all of the "close calls" he experienced, which provided him with God's preparation leading up to the *summum bonum* of his ministry, the protection of and provision for the House of

Jacob. So, in answer to his brothers' fears of his response to their malevolence against him, Joseph simply stated one of the foundational concepts of God's involvement with mankind. He told them, *"You intended to harm me, but God intended it for good to accomplish what is now being done, the saving of many lives."* (Genesis 50:20 NIV)

Whenever we experience the "close calls" of life, whether they be physical, emotional, psychological, or spiritual, God has purposes that far outweigh the temporal nature of the situation. Joseph was stripped of his "highly ornamented robe," was thrown into a pit, despaired of his life, was sold as a slave, was falsely imprisoned as an attempted rapist, and was ignored and forgotten for years in prison.

Yet just at the right time, God placed Joseph in the right place and worked a great work of grace in and through him that ultimately allowed God's people to survive and to prosper into a great nation.

Of course, we are not all Josephs. We'll not likely have a worldwide impact in some significant facet of civilization. But, like Joseph, we can be men and women of integrity; we can be one about whom it is said, "The LORD is with him." And we can allow God so to work in us that we are able, with a true spirit of forgiveness, to say to those who are vindictive and hateful to us, "You meant to harm me, but God meant it for good to accomplish His purpose."

When I was growing up there was only one "Hall of Fame." If someone was identified as being "in the Hall of Fame," he was obviously a baseball great. Today there are Halls of Fame for seemingly every activity and organization, no matter how obscure they may be.

But there still is only one "Hall of *Faith*," the eleventh chapter of Hebrews. And it is thrilling to me to see that, along with Abel and Noah and "the Patriarchs" and Joseph, and Moses, and David, and many other named heroes of the faith, there is a great number of unnamed men and women of courage who suffered intensely for their faith. It is these about whom the Bible says that they "gained approval through their faith."

We, the little guys of "the faith," are right there beside Joseph in God's "Hall of Faith," gaining the approval of God through our faith. And, interestingly enough, the writer of Hebrews closes the "Faith Chapter" by declaring the importance of our connection with the "Heroes of the Faith" in that, until we join them, they would not be "perfect [complete]." *"These were all commended for their faith, yet none of them received what had been promised. God had planned something better for us so that only together with us would they be made perfect."* (Hebrews 11:39-40)

Whatever "close calls" life has for you and for me, there are reasons and there are purposes...some found only in the heart and mind of God. But, like the arduous trek of Joseph to the position which would allow him to preserve the embryonic "Children of Israel," many reasons and purposes, upon reflection, can be seen in the here and now.

Might you dodge the bullets of your life, and may you have just enough fuel to make it aboard the ship of your future, in order that God can accomplish His will in and through you. And maybe it can be said of you and me, perhaps as our epitaphs, as it was of the great King of Israel, *"David, after he had served the purpose of God in his own generation, fell asleep..."* (Acts 13:36 NASB)

5.

A TALE OF TWO…VOLCANOES

Mt. Sinai was covered with smoke,
because the LORD descended on it in fire.
Smoke billowed up from it like smoke from a furnace,
the whole mountain trembled violently.
Exodus 19:18 NIV

"It was a dark and stormy night…really!" And thus began the recounting of my involvement with two of the world's most famous natural phenomena, one of the past and the other of the present.

The occasion was "Faculty Preplanning," a two-day planning and professional advancement event held by and for the faculty prior to the beginning of each academic year at *Toccoa Falls College*, where I was an assistant professor of Christian Counseling for eight years. During one of those years in the decade of the nineties, I had been asked to bring the opening devotional for the faculty of this Christian liberal arts college. Though I am an ordained minister (as were many of the faculty members at that time, especially in the School of Bible and Theology and the School of Missions), I felt that, rather than simply another homily encouraging perseverance and commitment to our kids and our profession, I would draw from my aviation background to paint a picture of what we and our students face on a daily basis and the provision that God has made for us to meet the daily challenges. (By the way, although we understood very clearly that we were personally, professionally, and spiritually working with young adults, most of the faculty still felt a sufficiently paternal or maternal affection for those in our classes or other organizational or personal connections to often refer to them as "our kids.")

My devotional went something like this:

On this dark and stormy night, the *USS Shangri La (CVA-38)* with its embarked airwing was steaming off the west coast of Italy, just finishing the air operations for that day at about 2300 hours (11:00 PM). I was a senior lieutenant in my squadron (VA-81) and was on my second Mediterranean cruise following my combat cruise in the Vietnam theater shortly after completing flight training in 1964.

During this particular night and on this particular flight, I was the "duty tanker." On each launch and recovery cycle of approximately twelve to twenty aircraft (some from each of the attack and fighter squadrons), which would last from one and a half to two hours, one attack aircraft was fitted with an "in-flight refueling apparatus" (called a "buddy store"). This "buddy store" was a fuel tank carrying an extra 2,000 pounds of fuel that also had a propeller in front that, when activated, provided power to a small generator which then ran a fuel transfer motor and allowed a hose to deploy out to fifty or so feet behind the tanker. At the end of the hose was "basket," a steel-mesh array that opened out like a three-foot wide funnel, assisting the pilot to engage his in-flight refueling probe to the hose.

A pilot would contact the duty tanker during the operational cycle if he wanted to practice in-flight refueling or if, for whatever reason, he actually found it necessary to take on additional fuel. On one previous daylight tanker mission, due to calm winds in the area, the ship had to delay turning into the wind for the recovery, and I had about a dozen very thirsty aircraft all calling for refueling. Even though the "buddy store" had the capability of draining the fuel from the tanker's fuel tanks as well as having the 2,000 pounds of fuel in the store, at that time each plane wanted a thousand extra pounds of fuel, and I didn't have 12,000 pounds to spare. (Note—a gallon of jet fuel weighs about 6.8 pounds, but the number of gallons a plane may have aboard is not nearly as important as its weight. So fuel amount is always given in thousands of pounds, i.e., the pilot's call when rolling into the "groove" for an arrested landing consists of plane number, fuel amount, and acquisition of the "meatball" of the Fresnel Lens; example, "Decoy 302, 2.8, Ball.") So, with a judicious use of my On/Off switch on my fuel transfer control panel and a very firm, "That's all for you...who's next!," I was able to top off all the aircraft with about 500 pounds apiece for their landings and still had just enough to come aboard myself (the tanker is always the last aircraft to land). Although I thought I had just accomplished my mission as it was supposed to have been done, the CO of the ship thought enough of it to have written up a commendation for me.

But things were much different on this dark and stormy night. First of all, nobody wanted to practice tanking (night in-flight refueling is a very dicey operation), so I circled the ship for an hour and a half at about 10,000 feet without any takers at all. And then, when the recovery began, I dropped down to 3,000 feet so that I would be readily available in the event any of the aircraft had trouble getting aboard and needed to refuel in order to have enough to try again. That was standard procedure.

What happened next was anything but "standard procedure."

The captain of the carrier, having been briefed that the carrier was steaming toward the southeast-to-northwest diagonal coastline of the western coast of Italy, reckoned that the ship was getting too close to dangerously shallow water. And, since there were only two aircraft still airborne, an F-8 Crusader and, of course, me in my A-4 Skyhawk, the Skipper decided to "bingo" (divert an aircraft to a land-based airfield) the two of us to the nearest airport ashore. That happened to be Capodichino Airport at Naples, now called Naples International Airport.

Uh oh! Periodically, sloppy preparations and a lack of professionalism born of complacency can catch up with a pilot and deliver a stinging blow. This was one of those times. Relying on the simple mission of the duty tanker, having hundreds of carrier landings under my belt, a fourth of them at night, and simply not being attuned to the range of possibilities I could be faced with, I hadn't planned a trip ashore and hadn't even looked at the information about the nearest airfield.

That really shouldn't have been too much of a problem, even as throat-tightening as the night and the storms were and now the reality of having to shoot an approach into an unfamiliar airport with English-as-second-language controllers in charge. No, the problem was something much larger. The problem was Mt. Vesuvius!

Mt. Vesuvius was a 4,200-foot volcano, just 10 miles east of the Capodichino Airport. My wife and I had driven to it on one occasion when she and several other squadron wives were over "chasing the ship" around the Med for about five of the nine months we were on cruise. The wives would go to our next liberty port while we were at sea, scope out the places of interest to visit, have fun among themselves until the ship arrived, and then we would spend an exciting week or so enjoying our wives' company in very exotic ports of call from Barcelona to Istanbul. "Join the Navy and see the world." Indeed!!

Anyway, on that occasion as we drove toward the

volcano, I noticed just how close Vesuvius was to the airport, just how high it jutted out from the sea-level port of Naples, and just where it was in relationship to the coastline. All of this flooded back to my memory as I tried to get my head together while flying in and out of the thunderstorms, while trying to establish radio communications with the flight controllers at the airport, and while dialing in the TACAN channel which would give me the distance and bearing to the airport. I'm afraid at that point my head wasn't coming together very well at all!

You see, it was that bearing to the airport that bothered me as I visualized our ship's position and the position of Mt. Vesuvius in relationship to the Naples airport. As best as I could tell, Vesuvius was directly between the ship (and therefore my position) and the airport...and the controller had me flying directly toward it!

I tried to be calm about it. After all, *he* knew there was a volcano out there I had to assume! But, I just couldn't shake the belief that, at the inbound bearing he had me flying, I was going to contact the volcano about 500 feet or so below the summit. Again, the volcano was precisely (in those days) 4,190 feet high, and I was flying at 3,500 feet. The ship had been steaming about a hundred miles south of Naples, but we had been steaming toward the coast for the entire hour-and-half of the operational cycle...and that, by my dead-reckoning, had put us southeast of Naples, sufficiently so that Vesuvius, with its close proximity to the airport, now lay in my path to the airport. And, since I couldn't see outside the cockpit because of the weather, I was not able to tell what my approach to the city looked like. I simply had to trust the controller not to run me into anything!

Just then, (with what I most likely mistakenly perceived as an "urgency" to his voice) the controller said, "Decoy 300, climb to 5000 feet!"

He didn't have to say it twice! Full power! Stick pulled

back in my lap! Going straight up! When I finally caught my breath and looked at my altimeter, I couldn't believe it! I was streaking through 10,000 feet, obviously on my way to the moon!

"Uhhh, Naples Control, Decoy 300...say again my altitude."

"Decoy 300, that's 5,000 feet."

"Rrrrroger, Naples Control...5,000 feet." Sheepishly, I reduced power, rolled my aircraft over to get the nose finally pointed down, and began a descent from wherever I was by now in the atmosphere back down to 5,000 feet, fervently hoping against hope that I didn't bump into anyone on the way down as I passed through what must have been many other aircraft's holding altitudes. I broke out of the clouds still out to sea as I approached the airport and made an uneventful landing with no other problems. But, I surely felt like a dunce, and the only thing that kept me from most likely being grounded for my folly was that I just didn't bother to tell anybody about my misadventure.

And to top it all off, the ship's steaming during the operational cycle of my flight had actually been more north than east. Thus, when I left the ship inbound for Naples, I was far more north and west than I had assumed. So I was never in any danger, and the closest I got to Mt. Vesuvius was the ten miles away it was when I landed. Dummy!

My next encounter with a volcano was far more pleasant. And it was almost directly south of this incident by a couple of hundred miles, just on the east coast of Sicily, the "football" that is being kicked by the "boot" that is Italy.

Later in the same cruise, the ship was again sailing in the Tyrrhenian Sea off the west coast of Italy. (We put into Naples a great deal because of the American naval facilities we have in Naples).

Once again I was flying a night hop, but this time there was no drama...at first. My mission was very simple. In order to assist the ship's technicians in calibrating one of the ship's radars, I was supposed to go out to a hundred miles from the ship on a certain bearing and return at a specified airspeed and altitude (about 20,000 feet). That whole operation only took about half of the operational cycle.

But I had noticed something at the far end of my flight away from the ship. The bearing from the ship that I was to have flown was in the southeast quadrant. And at a hundred miles from the ship, I saw something at a distance beyond me that I couldn't quite figure out. It appeared to be glowing, and it appeared to be shooting off fireworks.

Then I realized what it was! It was Mt. Etna. Mt. Etna was about 11,000 feet high...and Mt. Etna was erupting! It had been all over the news. Now that's drama!

With almost an hour to kill before I had to be at my "marshal point" to begin my approach to the ship, I decided I wanted to see down inside a volcano. That sounded like a gas; pun fully intended. So, I started back toward Sicily and contacted the flight controllers there. I told them that I'd like to see their volcano up close and personal and asked if that was possible. The controller I was talking with sounded like he thought I was nuts, but allowed as how he assumed it would be OK, if I stayed up above 20,000 feet...so that I would be out of harm's way. I gave him scout's honor and proceeded toward the volcano. It was getting to be more impressive by the minute.

As I crossed the northern coast of Sicily, the volcano was really all I could see. Rising gracefully more than half way to my altitude as a delicate cone ascending out of a placid range of mountains was majestic enough. But then sensing that there was more as I approached, I began to hold my breath... because I was certain that this was going to be breathtaking. That doesn't even come close to describing what I saw next.

Choosing not to fly directly over the crater at the top, I offset by a half a mile or so. And then, just as I reached my closest point to the opening, I banked the aircraft almost to 90 degrees to the right and began a tight circle so that I could see clearly out of the unobstructed side of the canopy, looking directly down into the middle of the volcano. There are hardly words for what I was seeing! It simply was amazing!

There was this brilliant, angry, roiling mass of molten lava, visibly churning around! I wondered right then as to how many people on earth had *ever* seen what I was seeing at that moment...and then lived to talk about it. It certainly couldn't be many, I thought.

And then it happened! As I was lost in the wonder of the majesty I was witnessing, the volcano gave me a private fireworks display. All of a sudden, several huge globs of flaming molten lava shot up toward me, looking for all the world like some of the antiaircraft fire I had experienced in Vietnam. Only this sight was never unnerving to me, since it became apparent almost immediately that the lava was slowing down and wouldn't reach my altitude (a silent prayer of thanks for the wisdom of the controller and my scout's pledge).

Slowly, about halfway up to me, the brightly glowing lava stopped, appeared suspended in mid-air for a few seconds, and then began a leisurely retreat to the side of the crater to join a flaming river of glowing lava twisting and turning down the side of the volcano. Years later, in the final scene of the movie, *Field of Dreams*, I saw a startling resemblance to this river (or highway) of lava. In the movie, cars were lined up at night for miles and miles into the distance forming a serpentine highway of indistinguishable lights in the darkness as far as the eye could see. That was just a part of the indelible memory of my awe-inspiring glimpse into the hellish beauty of the heart of a volcano.

My conclusion that day for the faculty in drawing these two episodes together was both mercifully and surprisingly (for me) succinct and to the point. I suggested that God had given us as teachers the privilege and the grave honor of gazing down into the turbulence of the adolescent and young adult mind and heart, and sometimes even into the tumult of their souls. At the time of life when there is often an angry and churning interior hidden in the placid exterior of the typical, standard-brand college student, we professors had been called upon to minister to those who often were still in the process of discovering who they were and to virtually all of whom were attempting to discover what it was that they would be willing to give their lives for in their future. And often in that process some shot the "fireworks" of frustration, of fear of inadequacy and failure, of loneliness and rejection our way, which sometimes came uncomfortably close to our own personal concerns. But that, in part, was precisely why their parents had entrusted them to us, to help them through the confusion, through the angst, and through the constant struggles of those years.

And though we may have fairly easily seen the emotional, intellectual, and spiritual turmoil of their struggle, all too often the ways to assist them became as murky as finding our own ways often had been. I mean, how were we to help some twenty-year-olds through the emotional and spiritual crises of their lives, when we were not always entirely able to see clearly our own way through the haze and fog of life.

That, of course, is a great part of the glory of our relationship with God through Jesus Christ. We don't have to always be able to see clearly to make it home safely. Our journey may be on "a dark and stormy night," and we may have no idea what lies ahead, except that we do know that there are possibly destructive obstacles embedded in the storm clouds of life. Aviators, by the way, often call those "embedded obstacles," *cumulo granite*, and running into one can ruin your whole day!

But the promise of the Word of God is that, even though *we* can't always see where we're going and what lies ahead, *God* has us clearly on *His* "radar." The Psalmist in the 139th Psalm reminds us, *"If I say, 'Surely the darkness will overwhelm me, and the light around me will be night,' even the darkness is not dark to Thee, and the night is as bright as the day. Darkness and light are alike to Thee."* (vv. 11-12 NASB) And Isaiah informs us as well of the power of the Holy Spirit for guidance when we're not certain which way to turn. *"Although the Lord has given you bread of privation and water of oppression, He, your Teacher, will no longer hide Himself, but your eyes will behold your Teacher. And your ears will hear a word behind you, 'This is the way, walk in it' whenever you turn to the right or to the left."* (Isaiah 30:20-21 NASB)

One night I looked down into the very heart of a tempestuous, agitated reality; another night I could see nothing, nor could I find my way to safety. But I learned that, no matter the turmoil and turbulence, I was able to fully trust the One who *could* see through the murky gloom and who *could* quietly guide me safely home.

And that's what I discovered that I could pass on to "our kids."

6.

THE JOY OF…AVIATION

Those who hope in the LORD…will soar on wings like eagles.
Isaiah 40:31 NIV

We all likely have heard the oft-quoted description of this job or that profession as being "hours of sheer boredom punctuated with minutes [or, perhaps, seconds] of sheer terror." And some may wonder if that's how I feel about aviation. Nothing could be farther from the truth. Aviation (at least in high-performance jet aircraft) is *never* boring. As someone has so wisely observed, "Mankind has a perfect record in aviation; we have never left one up there!"

You see, there is always this lingering understanding in the pilot's mind that, as soon as he takes off, sometime soon in his near future, that plane is going to come back to earth, either intentionally or undoubtedly in some unacceptably accidental way. Therefore the pilot to some degree is ever attentive to that fact.

In addition to the reality of the "Rule of Gravity vs. Flight"—*At some point in a flight, gravity wins!*—the pilot also should keep in mind (I say, "should," because many pilots do not) the limits of what he can do with his airplane. There have been far too many accounts in the past of pilots deciding to buzz their family's or their girlfriend's house to prove that, "Eighteen months ago I couldn't even spell 'aviator'. Now I are one!" So the hot-dogger makes a high-speed pass over the farm house, does a whoopsedoodle after the family has all run out to see what that noise was, and then finds out a tad too late that the back end of the whoopsedoodle requires a couple of hundred feet more than he had given himself above the south forty. Thence, the phrase, "He bought the farm!" That's certainly a tragic way to entertain the folks with his aviation prowess. Perhaps his epitaph should read the Forrest Gumpism, "Stupid is as stupid does."

So, within the constraints of appropriate attentiveness to the flight parameters of the aircraft and reasonable caution in the control of said airplane, there has been many an occasion in which I was in full wonder that I even asked the navy to pay me when I was out flying. Not every flight was explicitly life threatening, and not every flight made me feel that there was not enough money in the navy's budget to *ever* make me do *that* again! So I just thought it might be good to shift gears for a bit and to describe some of the pleasant, exhilarating, and even flat-out fun times I had in the cockpit. I certainly can't touch on them all, because, as the national media knows, good news doesn't sell. But here's a sampler of the times that my choice to be a naval aviator was a thing of joy.

Some flights were exhilarating simply because they were milestones. Undoubtedly, the initial one of those was the first solo flight. It wasn't really that things *felt* different in the cockpit, it was that they *were* different. There was no instructor back there carping at every move and every mistake...and there was no instructor back there to bail you out in case you got into trouble. There was a magnificent sense of advancement, of accomplishment, and of achievement in knowing that you had been entrusted with the aircraft and with your own short-term destiny...and that you knew you could handle it.

Then, at every level of training, there was the "Final Final" announcement. In the Training Command in my day, when reaching "final approach," that portion of the landing pattern in which the aircraft is lined up with and approaching the runway ready to proceed to touchdown, the student pilots radioed the tower with their plane number and the fact that they were "on final." The tower would then clear them for landing or send them around if there was a problem on the ground.

But at the end of the last flight in the syllabus for that portion of training at a particular training base, the pilot was given a measure of grace when his radio call was instead, "Tower, this is One One Two, Final final!" The return call from the tower operator was often an understanding, "Roger, One One Two, Final final...and congratulations. You are cleared to land." My, how that brings a lump to my throat just remembering it.

Then, as stress provoking as the first carrier landing was, the first catapult shot was that much more exciting. Not knowing what to expect in terms of the "kick" of the catapult, I had built up an anticipation that I thought was certain to overwhelm the reality. Not a chance!

Rarely, in fact only on a few occasions on some very intense roller coasters, have I ever yelled in excitement. That day, sitting on the catapult, awaiting the power that would get my jet trainer up to take-off speed (about 140 knots) in the two to three seconds of the catapult stroke, I felt like a kid at the carnival. I was going for a ride; I just didn't know how much of one.

Then, BAM! I was off!

I was immediately pinned back in my seat with the unexpected force of the catapult. The force was such a blast that I began yelling at the top of my lungs, *"Yaaaaaaaaaaaaaaaa"* all the way down the catapult track and off the front of the carrier until I managed a triumphant *"Hooooo!!"* as I climbed to 1200 feet and began my left turn to join the pattern for another trap and cat shot. It was amazing! I couldn't stop laughing it was such an extraordinarily thrilling experience. I knew from that day on that carrier operations were going to be at the very top of the most exciting and exacting accomplishments in my life.

Other flights had significance primarily for what they symbolized as well, but many of them were so involved with the most stressful aspects of the flying that they will have to be addressed at another time. Those flights had to do primarily with combat flying and/or arrested landings, the general trademark of the carrier pilot. Just as two men may ask each other their professions so that they can estimate where they match up on the pecking order, it's much easier for carrier pilots. If you hear an aviator state that he has 1200 carrier landings, you do an automatic, "Ooooooooooo!!" That's very impressive! So, every arrested landing giving a pilot a multiple of one hundred landings is a special event. His first hundredth landing makes him a "Centurion," the next, a "Double Centurion," etc. I was just short of being a "Quadruple Centurion," which was about the average for pilots finishing their first sea-duty tour. And, I was close to being a "Night Centurion"; that's impressive indeed, if only because every night "trap" should equal at least ten day "traps."

These figures and concepts take on added significance, I believe, when the results of one scientific study was reported after the Vietnam War. It seems that some navy flight surgeons serving on the carriers during the war decided to wire up a number of pilots so that they could check their vital signs throughout a few combat missions. They were looking at respiration, heart rate, perspiration, blood pressure, and other easily measured items. What they found was astonishing...especially to those of us who had been there.

They found that there were, in general, three spikes in the measurements of the flight...during the catapult shot, during the attack on the target, and during the approach and arrested landing. The cat shot was the lesser of the three spikes.

But to everyone's surprise, almost unanimously it was discovered that the vital signs were much higher *for the arrested landing* than when the pilots rolled in on their hot targets ("hot" here does not signify "sexy"…it means that the bad guys were doing their darnedest to do us in before we returned the favor). And the tests were only run for daylight missions. I can only imagine what the readings would have been for a truly dark night approach. They likely would have blown out the recorders!

But enough about flights, no matter how exhilarating, which were important simply because of their distinction. There were others that I had—and each pilot is fortunate to experience at one time or another—that were a delight simply because of their aesthetic character. We just happened to fly somewhere where it happened to be especially beautiful. Sunrises over the Caribbean with "the rays of the sun filtering through golden clouds, slowly bringing out the azure sparkle of the aquamarine lagoons that are framed by a white swath of beaches and surrounded by forest-green islands" immediately qualify. (Yes, yes…I know. That all sounds like a line from a travel brochure, quite a bit over the top…except that, if you've seen it, and that's how it looked, it truly was gorgeous. And I've seen it, and that's precisely how it looked.)

Once while flying commercially I had an experience of unusual beauty and stunning contrasts that I'll slip into this narrative. The flight was from Durango, Colorado to Denver one year in the middle of autumn. Since Durango is in extreme southwest Colorado and Denver is in the northeast, the flight path was almost entirely over the Rockies. The snow was early that year in the high country, so the mountains above the 10,000-foot level were entirely snow-covered and magnificent! The valleys were still clear, but from 25,000 feet, there was nothing as far as the eye could see but the snow-covered Rockies.

But as we approached Denver, leaving the "purple

mountain majesties" and began to let down "above the fruited plain," I noticed how colorless the entire area was; everything was just a drab, brownish blah! And that was everything, parks, farmland, business and college campuses...everything *except* two brilliant emeralds in a sea of dull sepia—Coors Field and Mile-High Stadium, the homes of the Colorado Rockies (of Major League Baseball) and the Denver Broncos (of the National Football League). Major League Baseball was just winding down, and Pro Football was in mid season...and those two fields were kept so green they dazzled the eye even at 15,000 feet. I think that says something about our societal priorities.

Let me tell you about three particular hops I remember that still take my breath away. The first was a trip from east to west along the entire length of the island of Crete in the Mediterranean Sea. I really don't remember the reason for the flight; I think it was just one of those opportunistic events that came up when my hop had a short mission and a long delay before the recovery began. But the amazing thing about Crete is that it has a mountain range down the middle of the island with at least three peaks above 7,000 feet—two of them at just about 8,000. Now that certainly doesn't sound like much after having flown over the Colorado Rockies (the mountains, not the baseball team) in which there are fifty-four mountains 14,000 feet high or more. But the island of Crete is about 140 miles long and only about 35 miles wide at its widest point! Those mountains look like they jut straight up from the sea, whether looking up from sea level or down from the peaks.

I began my flight at sea level, so that I could see what the mountains looked like while looking up at them. They were awesome! And then flying through some of the valleys and up around the towering peaks was equally as picturesque, since it looked as though the sides of the mountains plunged straight down to the sea.

And then to top the flight off (as though it needed icing on the cake), there are two prominent peninsulas at the extreme northwest corner of the island. As I exited the western edge of Crete, I began a climb to 30,000 feet for my cruise back to the ship, which was about 150 miles to the west. On one of the peninsulas the Cretans were doing some major excavation of some sort (mining perhaps?), which appeared to cut a broad swath across the peninsula. At about a hundred miles away I looked back to bid farewell to the island and was amazed to still be able to see that peninsula and the bright band across it through the haze from that distance. That was quite a flight.

But one other travelogue flight upstaged the *Tour de Crete* flight, and that was my own, personal *Tour de France* low-level excursion; this time compliments of a Franco-American joint military exercise. My assigned mission was to fly a particular track deep into southern France from the ship's position southwest of Marseille. I was to "coast in" north of the Pyrenees Mountains, which separate France from Spain, and head slightly west-northwest past Toulouse toward Bordeaux in the lush low country of southwest France. My briefing called for me then to proceed as far west as possible on the low-level mission until I needed to return to the ship because of fuel requirements.

But the trip up the river at about 3,000 feet was simply remarkable! I would pass over villages that from the air could still have been medieval, some with walls still around them, most with a castle on the highest point of land in the area. In fact, early in the flight my 3,000-foot altitude restriction still allowed me a very close peek at the local castles since the hills on which they were built climbed nearly a couple of thousand feet high. Those villages and castles and I got up close and very personal.

The entire low-level flight (flown at a slower than normal airspeed, since I had the time and *really* wanted to enjoy the view) was such an incredibly rare and marvelous opportunity to see an absolutely gorgeous portion of France from an unparalleled vantage point, that, as you can tell, I struggle even nearly four decades later to find the superlatives to describe it. I've never experienced anything quite like that flight in all my travels in the Mediterranean area, in the Caribbean, in the Far East, or in the U.S. It was unique in every sense of the word.

And only one flight in my memory ever topped it, and that was because it was not only beautiful, it was a whole lot of fun. On another occasion off the carrier (and I don't really remember where we were, nor does it matter to the story), I had a do-what-you-wish-to-do-for-most-of-the-hop mission. So I finished the minor task I was required and then climbed to altitude to conserve fuel. But, as I got away from the ship and continued my climb, I saw some intriguing cumulus clouds with puffy tops from 30-35,000 feet…and they were just begging me to come play. Who could pass that up?

I got up on top just to look around. What I saw was that in part the clouds formed what looked like mountains (with rounded tops) interspersed with valleys. Some distance away the cloud had more of a roughly flattened top that just seemed to drop off on the sides. Like a little kid at a children's park, I couldn't decide what I wanted to do first.

The mountains and valleys won out. Here was my chance to do all of the winding in and out between the walls of the cliffs on either side, whizzing past the peaks, and climbing precipitously at the last minute while speeding toward a ridge…all the flight "chase-scenes" one sees in a space or aviation adventure movie that nobody, but nobody in real life and in their right mind would ever do unless their life depended upon it, and their life certainly would be in jeopardy if they actually flew like that. But on this day I could do all of these maneuvers at full speed with no fear whatsoever of slipping up and making a fatal miscalculation. My mountains were very visible and yet totally forgiving.

I must have played in those things for half an hour, having more fun than any kid at a playground. But, with some sort of time and fuel constraints, I just had to get over to the other area of the cloud tops that looked for all the world like a snow-covered mountain top, five miles across and dropping straight down to the water from 30,000 feet. So I skimmed the top of the cloud right at "ground level," periodically scraping off the slight billows that were forming. But the thing I most wanted to do, I left for last.

When I was finally going to have to leave the playground and go back home, I began a wide circle right at the level of the cloud top. As I picked up air speed, I reached the farthest point along the cloud away from where I was going to exit. I turned toward the edge I had scoped out and began to fly toward it. At about half way there, I rolled the aircraft until I was inverted, flying just feet above the top of the cloud, now at about 500 mph. I steeled myself as I approached the edge of the cloud.

As I reached the cloud's end, I pulled as hard as I could, giving myself the impression I had run off the edge of a 30,000-foot cliff and was now plunging straight down to a watery grave. And I must admit…as much as I knew what I had done and the fact that it was just an illusion caused by my having been looking completely through the "top" of the canopy (since I was inverted) as I "fell" off the cliff, nevertheless, I scared the bejeebies out of myself! As I cleared the cloud (which looked amazingly like snow-covered ground) and saw how far down it was, my mind said that I was free falling and that I was "done for." The old "scared down in my tummy" feeling my four-year-old once described to me after a close call in the truck I was driving skidded on some ice was exactly what I was feeling as I continued in my plunge off the ledge. It was great!

Finally I just had to pull out of my dive to prove to myself that I was still actually in the airplane with a modicum left of control! I'm sure that there is no amusement park ride anywhere in the world that can come even close to that spontaneous thrill that I experienced that day...but if you could find one, you'd pay at least a couple of bucks for the chance to try it, and you'd probably only do it once!

Naval aviation, especially the high-performance carrier-jet branch of it, is inherently dangerous. But, as well, it is inherently challenging and exciting and, at times, even exhilarating. For those who have had the opportunity to face the challenges and to experience that exhilaration, there may be a few more stress lines in the face and gray hairs turning before their time, but there are even more and greater and lasting memories forged in the furnaces of challenges overcome and of limits surpassed, of duties accepted and of missions accomplished. In many ways the real joy of aviation lies in these memories.

But, at least in my own life, there is one more critical element that enriched the joy of aviation for me and that formed the foundation for the narratives of this book. That is my Christian faith.

From Ground School 101 on the first day of the Naval Aviation Training Command until my last flight in VA-113, when I came to realize that too many "close calls" and "near misses" had sapped the necessary intensity and dimmed the requisite focus to fly the exquisitely fine and demanding character of carrier aviation, I felt buoyed and borne along by more than simply my own performance capabilities. I experienced an awareness, even in the cockpit, of purpose and direction beyond that of simple mission focus and responsibility. I realized a peace "that transcends all understanding" (Philippians 4:6 NIV), especially after the events of September 20th, 1965. And I realized that faith in God through a personal relationship with Jesus Christ was as comforting as any controller's soothing guidance through the "dark and stormy night"; it was as protective as the ejection seat escaping an exploding aircraft; it was as steady as an <u>OK</u> 3 pass (the absolute best grade for an arrested landing...no mistakes whatsoever). That faith in God allowed this most junior officer in the squadron, when we first were confronted with surface-to-air missiles against us, the confidence to place the Philips New Testament translation of Ephesians 6:16 on the squadron white board in the ready room. No one seemed at all in a hurry to remove this admonition, *"Above all be sure you take faith as your shield, for it can quench every burning missile the enemy hurls at you."*

Naval Aviation for me was a profession, one that required study, hard work, intense focus, and great energy. I approached it in the same way I had my years at the Naval Academy; the same way, subsequent to my active duty naval service, I have in my years of ministry as a pastor, a counselor, a professor, and often "an all-around handyman." I have approached them all with dedication, determination, and real delight.

This trek through life, with a growing faith in God since I was a child, has resulted in a firm Biblical "hope" (full confidence in God for the future). And Isaiah the Prophet has reminded us that, *"Those who hope in the LORD...will soar on wings like eagles."*

What immeasurable *joy*!

7.

DON'T MISS THE BOAT

Enter by the narrow gate; for the gate is wide,
and the way is broad
that leads to destruction,
and many are those who enter by it.
For the gate is small,
and the way is narrow that leads to life,
and few are those who find it.
Matthew 7:13-14 NASB

The only thing worse than being catapulted off the *front end* of a carrier at night is the sure knowledge that two hours or so later you're going to have to bring it back aboard on the *back end* of that same carrier. And at that point you're exhausted and on edge and the night is infinitely darker and more hostile. Nothing ever quite prepares you for night operations from an aircraft carrier…not even day ops.

During the day when you are sitting on the catapult you have a panoramic view of the front third of the carrier and the horizon stretching from side to side as far as you can see. After you clear the ship your visual cues of the horizon, the sky, and the ocean make it easy to reprogram the violently reacting inner ears after the abrupt acceleration from zero to one hundred and sixty knots in about two and a half seconds.

But at night the visual cues simply disappear. While on the catapult there is nothing except the soft red glow of the flight deck (red lighting protects the aviator's and deck personnel's night vision) surrounded by an oppressive blackness that threatens to swallow up anyone foolish enough to challenge the night. The powerful roar of the engine at full throttle and the shaking and straining of the jet at the holdback, which keeps the plane from moving until the catapult fires, each contribute to the feeling that disaster is gleefully just waiting to pounce. And finally when both aircraft and pilot are thrust into the inky black, which has no up and no down and in which flight is felt but not seen, any slight movement of the head amplifies the confusion all five senses are experiencing as they do their best to believe the array of instruments which are telling you that you really are relatively safe, your plane is functioning normally, and that you are climbing away from the danger of an unforgiving sea which was just sixty feet below you as you cleared the flight deck.

But it is upon returning from your mission that the stomach really begins to churn and the mouth goes sandy dry. Because now you must point the nose of your aircraft *down*, towards the danger; you must fly back down to sixty feet above the water and attempt to put your jet down safely in a space about the area of a super-sized basketball court, all the while trying your best not to bounce off the back end of the carrier (the "ramp"), which is only fifteen feet or so below you when you pass over it at speeds varying from 130 – 150 knots, depending on your aircraft type. And you've got to do this with virtually no visual cues until the last couple of minutes of the approach.

At about five miles aft of the ship you begin to see the landing aids, the centerline strobe light and landing area markers that designate the safe landing zone. It looks for all the world like a miniature runway. But you know that's just the illusion the lights are designed to give. This is no runway. It is simply an area with four arresting wires spaced about thirteen yards apart. You put your aircraft down in that space…or you don't get aboard.

A lighted extension of the centerline drops down from the flight deck almost to the water level so that you can discern whether you're properly lined up or not. If there is any perceived bend where the "drop lights" meet the center-line strobe, you're off to one side or the other. Only when the drop lights appear in a straight line with the centerline are you properly lined up.

At about three miles you can begin to detect the Fresnel (pronounced "fra-nel'") Lens landing aid system (the modern update of the old "mirror landing system"). This aid, located on the port (left) side of the ship just forward of the landing area, shows you if you are on the proper glide path for landing. It does this by having a yellow beam of light that is visible above and below the three and one-half degree optimum glide slope in relationship to a horizontal row of green "datum" lights on either side of the lens. Thus, the lens shows that you are "high" on the glide slope if the yellow "meatball" appears above the datum lights or below the glide slope if the "ball" is below the datums. If the "ball" turns red (at the bottom of the system) then you are dangerously below the proper glide slope and are likely to crash into the ramp if you continue the approach at that rate. Flying the "ball" down to touchdown with it directly between the datum lights will put you exactly in the best place to land, just short of the third of the four arresting wires, not too close to the ramp, but still with two chances to catch a wire. In the accompanying photograph of what the landing area of a carrier's flight deck looks like from the cockpit, you'll note that the plane is slightly (half a "ball") high and is slightly right of the centerline.

The angled landing area of an aircraft carrier. The Fresnel Lens
is at center left. The arresting wires and center line are in the center;
the drop lights at center bottom. The LSO platform is at lower left
(where the crowd is). (Official Navy Photograph)

Also at three miles from the ship, where the lens' three and
one-half degree glide slope intersects the twelve hundred foot
altitude of the approach, the Landing Signal Officer begins
his visual observation and radio guidance of the aircraft. The
LSO, having observed thousands of "traps" (arrested landings), is able to provide the pilot with corrections often before
he (the pilot) even realizes that the corrections are necessary.
With a radio transceiver in one hand and control of the lens
lighting system in the other, the LSO can protect the pilot from
getting into irretrievable danger on the approach. A gentle,
"Power," when the pilot is going to get slow or, "No lower,"
when he's letting his aircraft get low on the glide path assists
the pilot to make timely corrections. Should the approach get
too dangerous or, for some reason should the deck not be
cleared for landing, the LSO commands, "Wave off! Wave
off!" and presses a button which flashes two vertical rows of

bright, red lights clearly warning the pilot to go around.

With all this help, bringing a high performance aircraft aboard a carrier at night still is the most emotionally demanding thing an aviator can do. The ship appears to be suspended in an all-encompassing pool of dark nothingness in which up and down are often meaningless. There is little sensation of movement and less ability to determine closure rate. In some ways the approach and the view of the carrier through the windscreen resemble a huge electronic video game…except that losing this "game" probably means losing your life.

In the last several seconds of the approach it becomes apparent that you are rushing toward the back end of the ship and that if you hiccup or twitch wrong you're liable to go low and get waved off or go high, land beyond the arresting wires, and continue on back into the night to try once again, but this time with a much tighter and drier throat.

It was in this extreme context, as a young pilot on my first Mediterranean cruise with my combat cruise behind me, that I nearly proved how easy it is to be distracted to death.

Having completed my mission of the night, I returned to the pre-briefed holding area aft of the ship, where the various aircraft had assigned distances and altitudes from the ship at which to fly their holding patterns. Each assigned "marshal point" was one mile more distant and one thousand feet higher than the one below it. The aircraft then would fly a left-hand racetrack pattern while in holding and were to leave the holding point exactly on the assigned minute, precisely one minute after the plane below, thereby automatically keeping a safe interval between descending and landing aircraft.

If, however, a pilot were to find upon his return that his radio was inoperative, there was also a pre-briefed holding pattern in a different sector from which the NORDO (NO RaDiO) would fly a *right*-hand pattern until the controllers on the ship noticed him on radar and assigned an aircraft to join up with him. That pilot would then fly the approach at the direction of the controllers with the NORDO on his right wing and would set him up – gear, flaps, and hook down, at 1200 feet, three miles, and on the "ball" – so that the NORDO pilot could then use the landing aids to guide him to a proper landing. The LSO could control him to some degree even without being able to talk with him by flashing the green "cut" lights (used to signal propeller-driven aircraft to cut power) on top of the lens apparatus if the NORDO needed power or by waving him off if he got dangerous.

I was the pilot on this particular night selected to bring in a NORDO. I was vectored to his position and joined up on him. I took the lead, got instructions from Approach Control, and began the descent. When we leveled off at 1200 feet, I flicked my wing lights to signal landing gear, flaps, and arresting hook to come down. At this point things were going famously. At three miles I had him on a centered ball, on speed for descent, and on centerline.

It was then that my second responsibility came into play. After breaking away to the left, my job was to parallel the NORDO's course about a mile away and at 1200 feet to insure that he made it aboard safely. If he didn't for some reason, I was to position my aircraft so that as he lifted off the angled deck he would notice me just ahead and above him. That way he could easily join up with me so that I could escort him around for another try.

There was just one problem on this particular occasion. I had become so intent on *his* approach that *my* aircraft was not only paralleling his course, it began as well to match his descent! With no external visual cues as to my progress and not checking my instruments periodically as all pilots are supposed to do (Dummy!), but instead locked onto his aircraft visually, I didn't realize that I was slowly settling toward the Mediterranean Sea. As the NORDO closed toward the ship, something began to "feel" wrong to me; I was simply uncomfortable without really knowing why.

And then it dawned on me! I was no longer looking *down* at the ship...I was looking *across* at it! Whereas the NORDO was about to stop safely when he landed on the flight deck, I had absolutely nothing to save me from destruction.

I quickly checked my altimeter. I was descending through 200 feet! In just a few seconds I would have settled right into a watery grave. As it was I jammed on full power, eased back on the stick, and caught my descent at about 150 feet. Climbing back to 1200 feet, I heaved a sigh of relief, whispered a prayer of thanksgiving, and marveled again at how quickly and unexpectedly we can exit time and enter eternity. By the way, the NORDO landed on his first try, and, after settling myself down, I came around to an uneventful landing...at least for a night trap.

How then, might all of this reflect spiritual realities of today? Well, far too many people in today's world feel that all they must do to be acceptable to God and to inherit eternal life is simply to live a good "Christian-like" life. They feel that it really doesn't matter what one believes, just as long as he lives a *good* life. That, to them, should be sufficient.

Jesus, however, implies in Matthew 7:13-14 that such an attitude is hogwash. He tells us that "the gate is *small* and the way is *narrow* that leads to life." There is a particular "Way" and a particular "Door." *"I am the Way..."* said Jesus, *"no one come to the Father but through Me."* (John 14:6 NASB) *"I am the Door; if anyone enters through Me, he shall be saved."* (John 10:9 NASB)

On that night out in the Mediterranean Sea, there were a multitude of places to fly an approach...to destruction. That gate truly was wide and the way certainly was broad.

But there was only one very small, very particular place one could fly down to safety. And that happened to be in the narrow confines of the landing area of the aircraft carrier and within the very narrow scope of the safe glide path.

An ironic aspect of the whole episode was that when I paralleled the NORDO's course and accidentally began to descend with him, I was flying a much smoother approach than he was. As an LSO myself, I could tell that. He was up and down, rough with his power and erratic with his wings. He barely got a passing grade from the controlling LSO.

But even though my approach was vastly superior to his, unfortunately I was flying mine in the broad way to destruction; he was doing his, however badly, in the narrow way to life. Again, all too many in today's world may say, "Well, I'm living better than that preacher (who ran off with his secretary) or that TV evangelist (who ran off with the payroll)." That may very well be true. But, ultimately it is *where* we live more than *how* (within prescribed boundaries) that is important. Or better said, *how* we live becomes important only when *where* is properly established. For, you see, Jesus said, *"He who abides in Me and I in him, he bears much fruit; for apart from Me you can do nothing."* (John 15:5 NASB)

Those who are in Christ (see Ephesians 1) may struggle, they may be up and down, they may be fighting difficult battles in their personal lives, their professions, or their ministries. Nevertheless, John 5:24 (NASB) tells us that they *"have passed out of death into life."* But tragically, no matter how "good" the one *outside of Christ* lives, he still is headed for destruction.

And without stretching this analogy too far, I believe I can suggest spiritual equivalents to the three "landing aids" which guide us down the "narrow way" and through the "small gate" to life.

The first is the Fresnel Lens, representing, of course, the Savior, the Lord Jesus Christ. It is this beam of light that penetrates the darkness to lead the helpless and lost airman to safety. It is *only* by flying down this glide path that the aviator can hope to get his plane down in one piece. That beam is "the Way" to safety. Should that beam be out, no matter how visible the ship may be and how comforting its presence, none could ever hope to come safely aboard without it.

The Scriptures clearly identify this guiding light:

The prophet Isaiah (9:2 NIV) tells us, *"The people walking in darkness have seen a great light; on those living in the land of the shadow of death a light has dawned."*

John the Beloved, in his Gospel, continues (1:4 NIV), *"In Him was life, and that life was the light of men."* And again (8:12 NIV), *"When Jesus spoke to the people, He said, 'I am the Light of the World. Whoever follows me will never walk in darkness, but will have the light of life.'"*

Paul the Apostle adds (II Corinthians 4:6 NIV), *"For God, who said, 'Let light shine out of darkness,' makes his light shine in our hearts to give us the light of the knowledge of the glory of God in the face of Christ."*

Secondly we have the centerline strobe light, which provides for the pilot the proper direction of landing and keeps him within the proper boundaries. It is imperative that the aircraft land on or very near the centerline in order not to break the arresting wire by placing too much strain near one end. As well, if the plane lands even fifteen or twenty feet off center, its wing may crash into other parked aircraft on the flight deck.

This certainly is analogous to the value of the Word of God in our lives. Just as it is the Living Word who guides us to life, it is the Written Word that provides for us the direction and parameters of the new life in Christ.

The Psalmist explains it like this (119:105 NIV), *"Your word is a lamp unto my feet and a light unto my path."*

Solomon puts it (Proverbs 6:23 NIV), *"For these commands are a lamp, this teaching is a light, and the corrections of discipline are the way to life."*

The Apostle Peter sums up (II Peter 1:19 NIV), *"And we have the word of the prophets made more certain, and you will do well to pay attention to it, as to a light shining in a dark place, until the day dawns and the morning star rises in your heart."*

And, finally we have the work of the Landing Signal Officer observing the aircraft and communicating directly with the pilot for guidance and evaluation. This naturally reflects the work of the Holy Spirit as He ministers in our lives. His work of convicting, empowering, guiding, teaching, comforting, and disciplining is integral in helping the struggling wayfarer to make it safely home.

Scripturally we see in Paul's letter to the Romans (8:16 NIV), *"The Spirit bears witness with our spirit that we are children of God."*

Ezekiel amplifies this (36:27 NIV), *"And I will put my Spirit in you and move you to follow my decrees and be careful to keep my laws."*

Once again in Romans (8:9 NIV) Paul says, *"You, however, are controlled not by the sinful nature but by my Spirit, if the Spirit of God lives in you."*

And then Isaiah (30:20 NASB) concludes, *"He, your Teacher, will no longer hide Himself...And your ears will hear a word behind you, 'This is the way, walk in it,' whenever you turn to the right or to the left."*

Father, our prayer is that no one among us or to whom we minister will ever have as his or her epitaph – "He flew a great approach; he just missed the boat!"

8.

"GET-HOME-ITIS"

How lovely are Thy dwelling places, O LORD of hosts!
My soul longed and even yearned
for the courts of the LORD;
How blessed are those who dwell in Thy house!
They are ever praising Thee.
Psalm 84: 1, 2, and 4 NASB

Get-home-itis – *def.* A malady, gender-specific to males, in which the desire to "get home" overrides all other concerns, including safety, comfort, and good sense. Usually preceded by "Get-*there*-itis," a similar pathology which only makes "Get-home-itis" even more bizarre, if that were possible. The primary symptom of these two illnesses is an inflammation of the neurological system which causes the individual to assume a hunched-shoulders, rigid, face-forward position while driving and keeps him from allowing any interruptions to this task, including stopping to eat, bathroom breaks, sightseeing, or (heaven forbid) stopping at a gift shop. An additional pathology often accompanies "Get-home-itis," known as "Compulsive Arrival Timing." In CAT the individual suffering with "Get-home-itis" predicts the time at which he will arrive at home, and, should he be more than a minute early or a minute late, he frequently becomes irritable, sullen, surly, and often infantile and childish. If he should arrive right on his predicted time, he may be seen dancing about the house shouting, "I'm number one! I'm number one!" There is no known cure for this debilitating syndrome.

The aviation form of "Get-home-itis" has one additional complicating factor. If the driver (the pilot of the airplane) makes any of the myriad mistakes possible during an acute attack of the disease (causing his vehicle to break down or run out of fuel, running into inclement weather in route or at his destination, etc.), he will not be able to stop, park the vehicle beside the road, get out, and wave down someone to get help. Instead, he will likely stall, spin, crash, burn, and die. Except for the ubiquitous "pilot error," "Get-home-itis" is the number one killer of aviators.

All pilots make fun of "Get-home-itis"; few pilots have missed getting into trouble because of it. I am *not* one of the latter.

My "Get-home-itis" adventure began rather innocently. While assigned to VA-81 stationed at NAS Cecil Field near Jacksonville, Florida in the spring and summer of 1967 between my two Med Cruises, I was detailed to take a junior pilot with me to a special assignment at Little Rock AFB, near (coincidentally enough) Jacksonville, Arkansas. This was a joint effort between all the major services, in which the army was testing some new radar and some newly-designed camouflaged field equipment, and air force and navy aircraft were to fly designated tracks to help the radar technicians to calibrate the radar, while, at the same time, attempting to determine how visible the equipment was from the air with low-level overflights.

The TDY (Temporary DutY) was for about a week, and it got the two of us out of the routine of the often-boring activities in between cruises. It was a good break, but when it was winding down, we were really looking forward to returning to hearth and home. You know what that led to.

Our first mistake was perhaps the most prevalent one in all "Get-home-itis" mishaps, leaving after a full day of work. Often the night before would have been a short one, with the desire to complete all the paperwork as much ahead of time as possible, the need to pack, and, for all too many, a chance for one more night on the town before returning to sense and sensibility.

The second mistake compounds the first...and that is that the preparation for the trip home is often rushed in order to get home as quickly as possible, with the real potential of missing something in the pre-flight briefing or the pre-flight inspection of the aircraft. It is confounding and really disturbing to see the disconnect in professional aviators at home and on TDY. They will take an hour to brief for a rather ordinary practice mission in a squadron setting and then will make a thorough pre-flight inspection of their aircraft prior to that flight.

But all too often, when away from the constraints of their regular professional structure, they will simply say, "We're going home. I'll lead; you follow. We'll go to channel four if we need to talk between ourselves. Otherwise, we'll be on the ATC-assigned channel. Any questions...good. Let's go." Then, without even their own maintenance personnel having set their aircraft up, the pilots often make a perfunctory pre-flight, consisting of "kick the tire, light the fire, and let's do it."

I really have little recollection of the extent of my briefing for my wingman when we ended our TDY back then and decided not to wait until the next morning to return home. Nor do I remember whether our pre-flight inspections were thorough or cursory. I'm hoping that I handled myself more professionally than the results showed, but I'm afraid the "Get-home-itis" was beginning its insidious work.

The third mistake is often the clincher in determining whether the homecoming is joyous or somber. All too often someone with this dreaded malady will simply ignore the warnings given him about the weather conditions in route or at his destination or both. It's almost as if his desire to get home will in some way magically disperse the clouds, dry the rain or melt the snow, and clear a path through the storm for the impatient and careless aviators. But magic like that hardly ever happens...except occasionally for a fortunate few...like me, for example.

However thorough or perfunctory our briefing, I know that I did not cover the airports to which we could divert in the event of bad weather closing our destination. I also didn't take into account the caution of the meteorologist who suggested that the thunderstorms in the Cecil Field area were picking up and becoming more widespread. After all, we faced flying everyday in the area of the most concentrated number of thunderstorms in a one-hundred-mile radius *in the world*...why should it bother us on this one night? (The answer was because we were already tired—therefore we would be exhausted at the end of the 700-mile, two-hour flight. As well, it would be twilight when we arrived, and though we would be OK on fuel if we landed there, should we have to divert from there for any reason, we would be in deep trouble.) We simply left ourselves no margin for error, and that was my responsibility...completely.

And then errors we got!

The first bad news passed on to us by the air traffic controllers was that our last bingo (divert) airfields (NAS Pensacola and, alternately, Eglin AFB) on the way over to Cecil Field or NAS Jacksonville were socked in because of bad weather. When we got that word, we were already well past other bases at which we could land in the event Cecil Field should go down. So throats began to get both dryer and tighter...a sure symptom of advanced "Get-home-itis."

As we continued to plunge into the gloom of the ever-darkening twilight to our east, my wingman pulled right up beside me and gave me hand signals that his radio was on the blink. Oh, great! Now, whatever needed to be done, I was going to have to do it thinking for both of us, since he would have no idea of what was occurring, except that it was my responsibility to get him home safely to his sweet little wife.

Then, as we approached home base, the worst news of all. A series of thunderstorms had already closed NAS Jacksonville and was moving in on Cecil Field. The tower told me that they expected to close the field in no more than ten minutes and then it would likely remain closed for an hour. That was *not* good!

I quickly began to compute my fuel to the nearest airfield the flight controller had told me was open, the airport at New Orleans. Even if we were to make it that far, we would be so critical on fuel when we arrived that it would be totally unprofessional to take two aircraft that were that low on fuel over a highly-populated area. I realized I simply couldn't do that.

There was a quick memory of a friend of mine who took a division of F-4's on a cross-country flight one time and made a mistake similar to mine. His flight got very low on fuel before they reached their destination. As he was trying to nurse them home, he was able to land successfully. But the other three aircraft all ran out of gas before they were able to land...and, unfortunately, not all the pilots were successfully able to eject. It was a sad situation all around.

So I was facing a real dilemma. Should I continue toward Cecil Field, in which case I would have plenty of fuel to either land immediately or to hold for a reasonable amount of time (but not for the hour that the controller had told me he would expect the field to be closed when the line of thunderstorms reached there). Or should I immediately try to find an open field close enough for me to take a wingman with no radio and a dark night creeping up on us. Rock...and Hard Place...and I was right between them!

By this time I had reached the field and had begun an orbit

right over it between cloud layers at about 3,000 feet. Evidently I needn't worry about other aircraft; they were all smart enough to have gotten back and on the ground a long time ago. As I circled I thought, and I figured, and I prayed ("Lord, I really need a break here, in the clouds, that is")…and I waited. The clouds below me obscured the field; the clouds above me were threatening to engulf the two of us. Nevertheless, I was pretty well committed to landing right here, right now.

We could shoot an IFR approach, but we just didn't have the time to have approach control take us out to a safe distance and get us set up for a radar-controlled approach. And, even if we did, I would have to bring my wingman down almost all the way to touchdown, drop him off, and then go around and make another approach. Although the air force had been making section landings forever, we navy types made section takeoffs, but we'd never tried landing with a wingman. And I didn't feel that this night with this weather would be the time to try my hand at it for the first time…especially with a wingman with no radio. So, I continued to circle.

With my wingman on my right while I was circling to the left, all of a sudden the heavens opened up! At least the clouds below me did…Hallelujah! Right below us was the tower and the runways, each as clear as a bell…except off the end of the duty runway there was a huge wall of water moving slowly toward the field.

Now was the time for a command decision!

"Cecil tower, I can see the field. My wingman is on his way down and will be first to land. His radio is out so he will simply taxi to our squadron area after landing. Please give him a green light for landing and for taxiing." I did *not* make a request to land. We were going to land. I'd deal with complaints later…when my feet were firmly and safely planted on the ground.

I turned to look at my wingman (it was barely light enough for me to see him and vice versa). Making very clear hand signals for him to look down at the field and then that he should break away and dive through the clearing in the clouds and land, I gave him the "Go NOW!" sign. Boom! He was gone!

And, boom! I was right behind him. Under the clouds at about 1,000 feet, things actually weren't too bad…except for that thunderstorm approaching the other end of the duty runway. It was going to be very, very, very close as to whether both of us would get down before the rain made landing impossible.

With the heavy rain encroaching on the landing area there were two immediate problems. The first for my wingman was whether the rain would reach far enough down the runway to cause him to hydroplane while he was trying to brake. That would mean that he would completely lose control of the aircraft…just as motorists do in their cars when they hydroplane. That problem would be even more extreme for me by the time I got down.

The second problem was more mine than my wingman's. When that rain got far enough down the runway, whoever ran into it would completely lose the ability to see outside the aircraft. My wingman was going to be on the ground and would likely be taxiing to our hangar. But I knew that I was going to get into it at some point; I was only hoping against hope that I would be on the ground first, and that I would be sufficiently slowed down that I could expect to get stopped without running off the runway.

As I was turning into the groove I saw my wingman make his landing and continue down the runway to a taxiway about two-thirds of the way down to the end. And then he just disappeared into the curtain of water. Good luck, fellow! I trust that I shall be so fortunate.

There was one very positive aspect of the thunderstorm that was approaching the middle of the runway by the time I reached the threshold…the wind off that sucker was powerful and right down the runway toward me. That meant that my over-the-ground speed was much slower than usual, which, of course, would mean that I could expect to slow down much more quickly and in much less distance than normal after I touched down.

In fact, I thought later of a situation that was an extreme example of what happened to me that night with the intense wind down the runway from the thunderstorm. A small plane, a Piper Cub or something along that line, was scheduled to land aboard an aircraft carrier for some publicity reason. The small plane's landing speed was about 40 knots. The carrier could steam at 20 knots and there was at least a 20-knot wind that day as well, so the Piper Cub (or whatever it was) flew toward the ship and then about half way down the flight deck, reduced its throttle to its normal landing power and hovered there in that 40-knot wind right over the deck. Slowly he settled straight down to touchdown on the flight deck. The pilot immediately cut his power and put his brakes on, and the plane never moved.

Well, that night in the wind and the rain, I had to do a great deal more than begin to hover over the runway. Nevertheless, my normal landing airspeed of about 125 knots translated that night to an over-the-ground speed of no more that 90 knots or so, with the 35 to 40-knot headwind that I landed into. I got on the brakes as soon as possible (I had to be careful not to blow a tire), and I began to slow quickly as I continued my landing roll down the runway.

But it became very apparent that I was not going to get off the runway before I ran into the curtain of rain. It looked almost deadly as I approached it, very much like a waterfall with a solid mountain behind it. But, when I plunged into it, all that I saw was the hardest rain I'd ever experienced. There was nothing out there but water. It was raining so heavily, I couldn't even see individual drops; it was more as if a faucet had been turned on.

But so far, things had gone pretty well for a couple of pilots who might just as easily have had to depart their aircraft somewhere along the line and then who would have had to have lived with the consequences for the rest of their lives. Of course, the primary consequences would have been mine.

But right then, at that moment, the only thing left to accomplish for us to get out of that whole affair smelling like a rose was for me to keep the aircraft going straight down a runway that I could no longer see. If I could do that until I stopped, I would be able to wait awhile right there in the middle of the runway, with my engine at idle, while the worst of the rain passed over. Certainly nobody else was going to use the runway during that time. Then, before the next cell approached, I could taxi to the hangar, and act as if we had planned the whole thing the way it turned out.

And that's just what happened.

As I reflected on my "Get-home-itis" journey, I remembered a delightful little movie of the late 80's entitled, "Saving Grace." Tom Conti plays a newly-elected Pope, who accidentally locks himself out of the Vatican while in his gardening clothes. Having been feeling for some time that he had lost touch with his people, he decides to use this time to journey to a village he had heard about which had no priest. There he found the village controlled by a sleazy bully who kept the villagers in bondage and fear. The story tells of how, through his personal intervention, the Pope, who had remained anonymous throughout his mission, was able to provide liberty, joy, and hope to the villagers. The movie was considered nothing more than a warm and rather harmless little story by the Hollywood establishment.

But Hollywood had been collectively hoodwinked. "Saving Grace" was actually a wonderful and moving allegory of Christ coming to earth, defeating the power of the evil one, and providing freedom, joy, and the hope of eternal life through his personal intervention on the cross. The movie even ends with the people of the village traveling to the Vatican to stand with the huge crowd of pilgrims in St. Peter's Square where they recognized their "visitor" as the Pope. This representation is, of course, the gathering of the saints before the throne of God in the heavenlies, with the Christ, God the Son, standing at the right hand of the Father.

I bring up this amazing movie, because it tells of an allegorical journey…and I realize that my "Get-home-itis" flight can also be seen as an allegory. It can represent the desire of the Christian, who really does want to reach his heavenly "home base," but who makes many mistakes on the journey, often jeopardizing himself and those around him. In a very truncated fashion, that flight was my own "Pilgrim's Progress."

But there is a Biblical allegory that is familiar to all of us with ultimately the same theme. The Psalmist assures us in the 100th Psalm that we are both God's people and His allegorical "sheep" in His eyes:

> *Make a joyful noise unto the LORD, all ye lands.*
> *Serve the LORD with gladness:*
> *come before his presence with singing.*
> *Know ye that the LORD he is God:*
> *it is he that hath made us, and not we ourselves;*
> *We are his people, and the sheep of his pasture.*
> Psalm 100:1-3 KJV

With that understanding, we can look, perhaps with new insight, into the "journey" of the Shepherd's Psalm, Psalm 23.

In the picturesque language of the Mid-East of a millennium before Christ, the Psalmist portrays himself as a sheep being led by the Heavenly Shepherd in the first part of the Twenty-third Psalm {presented here in the New American Standard Bible version}, in verses 1-3. In this picture, all of his needs are met and his life is tranquil and peaceful:

The LORD is my shepherd, I shall not want..
He makes me lie down in green pastures;
He leads me beside quiet waters.
He restores my soul;
He guides me in the paths of righteousness
for His name's sake.

But, at this point, the Psalmist begins to transition his thoughts from himself as a sheep to himself as a part of the people of God, as a division in the text in the NASB translation implies. Both the shepherd and the sheep would naturally be wary of the shadowy valley into which they were entering, where predators, both human and beast, awaited the careless traveler:

Even though I walk through the valley
of the shadow of death,
I fear no evil; for Thou art with me.
Thy rod and thy staff, they comfort me.

This valley of the shadow of death most likely was a narrow trail encompassed by high cliffs and craggy overhangs that kept the sun from reaching the valley floor. The dark caves and protruding ledges would provide hiding places and attack points for the predators. The evil for both the sheep and the shepherd would include the lion and the bear and other four-footed killers, which lay in wait for a prey to satisfy their appetites.

But in the same dark and gloomy confines, there also would be roving bands of brigands, who would think nothing of attacking a defenseless shepherd to steal his sheep, or even, as related by the Christ a thousand years later, nearly killing a hapless traveler, who ultimately would be tenderly ministered to and cared for by a despised Samaritan.

It was in this allegorical setting that the sheep must

depend upon the protection of the shepherd, and the shepherd must depend upon the power and might of the "Chief Shepherd" (I Peter 5:4), that "Great Shepherd of the Sheep" (Hebrews 13:20), the Mighty One who was *his* Shepherd, the LORD Himself.

And once having traversed the shadowy valley of predators, the individual would find, at the end of his journey, his reward and his exaltation:

> *Thou dost prepare a table before me*
> *in the presence of my enemies;*
> *Thou hast anointed my head with oil; my cup overflows.*
> *Surely goodness and lovingkindness will follow me*
> *all the days of my life,*
> *And I will dwell in the house of the LORD forever.*
> Psalm 23 NASB

I had taken a journey that summer day in 1967. I had passed through my valley of the shadow, and undoubtedly death had lurked there in many guises for my wingman and me. But in God's good pleasure and by His grace, we were spared from the then-present evil.

For each of us who claim "the LORD" as our shepherd, the journey continues. There are times of green pastures and still waters; there are generally many more days of dark valleys and physical, emotional, and spiritual predators seeking whom they may devour.

But the One who said, *"I am the good shepherd...and I lay down my life for the sheep,"* (John 10:14 and 15 NASB) is the One who has promised, *"And, lo, I am with you always..."* (Matthew 28:20 NASB). He is the One with the rod to drive off the evildoers. He has the staff with which to retrieve us from dangers and to nudge us along the "straight and narrow."

And it is He who finally ushers us out of the shadows

and into the eternal sunshine of His glory, to the table of delights and to the overflowing cups. It is He who will anoint us with the oil of His Spirit, and it is then that we shall echo the victory cry of all of those with spiritual "Get-home-itis": *"And I will dwell in the house of the LORD forever."* Amen!

9.

WHAT YOU DON'T KNOW *CAN* NOT ONLY HURT YOU, IT CAN ALSO RUIN YOUR WHOLE DAY!

No man knows when his hour will come…
So men are trapped by evil times that fall
unexpectedly upon them.
No one knows what is coming—
Who can tell him what will happen after him?
Ecclesiastes 9:12 and 10:14 NIV

It happened on the evening of our eighth wedding anniversary, June 6th, 1971…just a week after our daughter was born and four weeks before my plane crashed in the Sierra Nevada Mountains. It certainly was a terrible tragedy in itself, but the tragedy was compounded because it was so immanently avoidable.

"It" was a mid-air collision between a military jet and a passenger airliner. The pilot of the military jet was killed, though his RIO (Radar Intercept Officer) was able to safely eject. All forty-nine passengers and crew of the airliner died in the mishap.

A Hughes Airwest DC-9 departed Los Angeles International at about 6:00 PM that evening bound for Salt Lake City. At the same time a Marine Corps F-4B Phantom II was returning from NAS Fallon, near Reno, to the El Toro Marine Corps Air Station in Orange County. The planes collided over the San Gabriel Mountains at about 15,000 feet.

But here is the hyper-tragic part: Unsubstantiated reports alleged that the F-4 was doing unauthorized aerobatics in an unauthorized airspace at an unauthorized time. The pilot of the airliner likely never knew what hit him.

When I first heard the news of the collision, my initial thought was "Nearly been there; nearly done that." You see, a few months before, I had nearly become the first military pilot to bring down a...*Boeing 747*! And it was because of something that I *didn't* know that caused the responsibility for that "near mid-air collision" to be shifted from the 747 to *moi*.

Here's how it happened.

Lcdr. Jon R. Harris in the Spring of 1970
as a Company Officer at USNA
(Official Navy Photograph)

After leaving the Naval Academy following my two-year stint as a company officer, I was fortunate to get my first choice of both aircraft and duty assignment. I had asked for the newest navy attack aircraft, the A-7 Corsair II, and I'd requested to be assigned as an air wing LSO (Landing Signal Officer.) Such a position would be opening up very soon on the staff of the Commander of Carrier Air Wing Fifteen at NAS Lemoore, some 40 miles south of Fresno, California. So, after seven years of career and marriage always home-ported on the east coast, Patty and I packed up and answered Horace Greeley's turn-of-the-20th-Century admonition, "Go west, young couple, go west!"

Before I could begin my duties on the staff of the air wing, I had to complete the rigorous ground and flight training in the new aircraft I'd be flying. There are special squadrons in naval aviation which transition *new pilots* from the Naval Aviation Training Command, *more-experienced pilots* from other types of aircraft, or *any pilot* coming back into aviation from a non-flying billet into the fleet aircraft to which they've been assigned. These Replacement Air Groups (RAGs) train the pilots in the various systems of the airplane (electrical, hydraulic, propulsion, weapons, etc.), and how they integrate functionally. The squadron then takes the pilot through all phases of flight performance and combat training. Finally they conclude the preparation for the pilot with day and night FCLPs (Field Carrier Landing Practice), where the airfield is set up and used to represent a carrier's landing area, before they then try the real thing, day and night arrested-landing qualifications aboard the carrier. At the end of all of that, the pilot then finally gets to report to his squadron, or, as in my case, to the air wing staff.

But while I was in VA-122, the A-7 RAG at NAS Lemoore, I relished the introduction to the A-7. I had flown the A-4 Skyhawk on my first sea-duty tour of three cruises, a combat cruise to the Vietnam theater followed by two

Mediterranean cruises prior to my assignment to the Naval Academy. Having the opportunity to enter the A-7 community at the ground floor was very much a dream come true.

In many ways the A-4 was a "Model T" to the A-7's "Cadillac." The A-4 was undoubtedly the "most" airplane *for its size* in aviation history, the most maneuverable, the most flexible in armament and mission capability, the most cost-efficient, and, in a completely unbiased and, I'm quite certain, unanimous decision, the most fun to fly. You might remember the A-4 as the "adversary aircraft" flown by the instructors in the movie, *Top Gun*; the aircraft half the size of the F-14s that "whupped up" on them Tomcat drivers until they were taught "really" how to fly. Still, the A-4 was admittedly in some aspects simply upgraded from WWII aircraft primarily by its propulsion system, at least as it was configured when I was flying it in the mid to late 60's.

The weapons delivery system, for example, was exactly the same when I was diving on a target in Vietnam as it had been, nearly a quarter of a century before, in the dive-bombers that destroyed four of the six Japanese aircraft carriers from the attack on Pearl Harbor six months later at the Battle of Midway. The bombsight was the same, the critical need to release the bombs at the proper dive angle, air speed, and altitude was the same, and the "by-guess-and-by-golly" factoring in of the wind speed and direction was exactly the same. The only things that differed at all were that the power and air speed were greater in the jet than in the WWII-propeller-driven aircraft and the Vietnam-era GP (general purpose) bombs were now of a sleek, low-drag configuration, rather than the high-drag fat-bomb design of past wars.

Navigation in the A-4 in large part still depended upon the pilot's capability to discern landmarks on the ground vs. their representations on a map to confirm the present position and future destination. When climate or weather changes obscured the countryside—lakes drying up or ice and snow covering rivers and roads, the pilot very often was stretched beyond his limit to accomplish vital navigation.

But navigation and weapons delivery in the A-7 now entered the high-tech world of computers. The A-7 had the first on-board computer that I'd ever seen. And whereas the A-6 Intruders of VA-75 that the *USS Independence* first took to war in 1965 had computers, the A-4 was the last of the "smart pilots—dumb plane and bombs" in the fleet. The A-7, on the other hand, became the first single-seat, carrier attack jet to launch into the new age of computerized warfare.

The A-7's navigation system integrated its forward-looking radar with a computer-run map on a monitor. A cursor representing the aircraft moved along the map governed by the computer's generated flight path by incorporating the plane's sensors of the airspeed and direction of the plane coupled with the ambient wind speed and direction. Having typed in the precise longitude and latitude (which was painted on the tarmac at each plane's parking spot at the air station) immediately upon starting up the computer prior to taxiing out, the computer, even without today's microchips, was able to do a creditable job of maintaining a true spatial positioning throughout a three-hour flight.

The weapons delivery system of the A-7 was equally as radical for the former A-4 driver. Because of the computer's reading from the plane's sensors of the dive angle, airspeed, altitude, and wind speed and direction, the pilot only had to begin the dive, place the "pipper" (the computer-gener-ated crosshairs of the computer's bombsight) on the target and depress and hold the "pickle button" (the bomb-release button on the stick) throughout the bomb run. When the computer felt it was time and position was optimal for releasing the bombs, there would be a "clunk" (when the bombs were kicked off) and a jump of the airplane now free of the excess weight that indicated the bombs were away. Usually the placement on target was far more accurate than the average drop-radius of the A-4 at its best.

The only drawback I saw in the A-7 because of its upgraded technology was the tremendously increased demands placed on the pilot both for navigation and weapons delivery responsibilities. In the F-4 the pilot had the GIB (the "guy in back," more formally known as the RIO) to do much or most of the navigation and weapons set-up for him. The B/N (Bombardier/Navigator) did the same for the A-6 driver.

But in the A-7, every responsibility in the aircraft was the pilot's. That was both the bane and the blessing of flying a single-seater…there was no one else in the cockpit looking over your shoulder, but, equally as true, there was no one else in the cockpit looking out for you, either. Some days having someone there might have been a good thing.

One day in the midst of my flight training in the replacement squadron, I was scheduled for in-flight refueling practice. My scheduled take-off time was well ahead of the time I was to join up with the tanker and another flight of A-7's over the Sierra Nevadas. The tanker was to be flying from north to south over the Sierras just southeast of San Francisco.

As an experienced aviator, the operations folks in the squadron gave me some latitude in filling in the blank spots in my scheduled hops. If I were scheduled to be at a certain place at a certain time, they knew to expect that I would be there on time, so they really didn't care greatly what else I did on the flight.

What I decided to do that day was to head out directly west soon after taking off. While climbing out I would cross the San Joaquin Valley, over the Santa Lucia Range of mountains and highway US 1 right on the coast. I would then continue out to sea over the Pacific as I turned to the north. That course would start my "coastal sightseeing tour" just south of Big Sur, up to the Monterey Peninsula (Pebble Beach Golf Course and the city of Monterey), across Monterey Bay and north of Santa Cruz, where I was to turn to the east and coast in. That would allow me to answer that classic 70's pop song, "Do You Know the Way to San Jose?" I would be passing ten miles or so just south of that city.

Since I was now going east and was flying VFR (following "visual flight rules"), which we were still able to do in those days, I had to ensure that my altitude was correct. In the "upper airspace (above flight level 210—21,000 feet), all aircraft going from 000 – 179 degrees had to adhere to an odd flight level, i.e. FL210, FL230, etc.), whereas those going to the west had the even flight levels. This provided at least a 1,000-foot vertical separation for all aircraft in general.

So my responsibility was two-fold, to keep a good lookout since I was flying VFR, and to ensure that I was at a proper flight level for my direction. I was at about 20,000 feet as I coasted in, so I climbed to FL210. This would give me at least a 5,000-foot clearance when I reached the Sierra Nevadas as well.

At this point I also turned on my IFF (Identification Friend or Foe) Transponder, which sent out an electromagnetic signal that allowed the air traffic controllers to "see" the aircraft better on their radar amongst the clutter of the cities, mountains, and other aircraft. That is, it would have done that if the aircraft's IFF had been working, which I found out subsequently that mine wasn't. That was one component in an "almost" tragedy.

While I was cruising at altitude toward the rendezvous point with the tanker aircraft, I vividly remember thinking of how helpful the east-west flight-level segregation rules were working that day. I was seeing a *lot* of aircraft passing off to the side above and below me going the other way.

In fact, I just wanted to be certain that I hadn't accidentally climbed or descended significantly since I coasted in, so I checked the instruments (altitude—right on; airspeed— OK to get me to my join-up location on time; rate of climb or descent—zero; fuel on board—no problem; bearing—

directly to my rendezvous point). Everything looked good, even my position on the map on the computer, which I watched for a few additional seconds.

And then I looked up. Half of my heart sank; the other half leaped into my throat. I simply couldn't believe it…I was about to die!

There, stretching across the width of my bulletproof forward windscreen was a 747, heading directly at me, not a mile away! I knew precisely what it was in the instant I saw it…but there was absolutely *no* time to wonder where it came from or how it got there or why it was precisely at my altitude. I saw it, and if I didn't do something *right now*, I was dead, and, most likely I would do a much better job of taking the 747 down with me than the small plane did that crashed into one in the classic movie "Airport 75."

No thought; just reflexes! Snap roll to the left, pull for everything I was worth…one thousand one, one thousand two, and then reverse the turn! If I was still alive, then I should have missed him. I opened my eyes, and sure enough…I was passing along his right side; not close enough to see the passengers in the windows, but plenty close enough to see the big A/A on the tail. American Airlines. I think we both (I and the AA pilot) agreed at that moment with the wag who once said, "Never trade luck for skill." I'll say "Amen" to that!

After I quit shaking, my mind now had time for those questions, "Where *did* that plane come from?" "How *did* it get there without my seeing it?" "Why *was* it at my altitude going west?!" Now I was starting to get angry.

I still had a scheduled task to carry out, but you better believe that I was going to get to the bottom of all of this!

After the in-flight refueling and then returning to the base, I stomped up to the operations office and told the duty officer what had happened. He could see that I was visibly upset and suggested that I call the regional office of the Federal Aviation Administration. Good idea!

I checked my flight plan again just to make certain that I was clear of applicable restricted areas during my flight, and all the available charts showed that I was. When I got an FAA staff member on the phone, I told him what had happened and that it had been an American Airlines "widebody" that tried to do me in. I gave him my position and the time of the incident and asked if he knew why the aircraft would have been at my flight level even though he was heading west. And then I wondered why no one had warned me about a plane in my vicinity. He told me that he'd look into both and get back with me.

In the meantime I began to crunch some numbers: Let's say that the 747 was approaching one of the major airports behind me, either San Francisco International or even San Jose International. He likely was slowing down, so he could have been at 300 knots. I was cruising at 350 knots. That would have been a closing speed in miles per hour of roughly 720 mph. A quick running of the numbers told me that we were rushing toward each other at twelve miles a minute or a mile every five seconds! In the fifteen or twenty seconds I had my head in the cockpit checking my instruments and watching my progress on the computer, we had closed from four or five miles down to one. But just before I looked in the cockpit, I had been watching a plane passing off to my left and a thousand feet above me like he was *supposed* to be!! So I really hadn't looked ahead of me for probably half a minute or more. The 747 would have been over six miles away the last time I could have seen him. But, since he was heading directly toward me, I easily could have missed the least-visible straight-on view, and undoubtedly I was too small for him to see.

So, when I looked up, and immediately broke left, counted to two and rolled out, that five seconds put us right beside one another, separated by no more than a couple of hundred feet. Much, *much* too close for comfort!

The FAA official called me back to verify my position and time...and then to explain the mystery. He talked with the only American Airlines 747 pilot airborne at that time. The pilot said he was descending for an approach into San Francisco International, and *he never saw another plane.*

"Descending for an approach?!! What was he doing descending through my airspace? He almost got us all killed!" The FAA official was very patient with me all the way through my tirade.

"LCDR Harris, he wasn't in your airspace...you were in his."

"Huh?"

"Yes, I'm afraid that you were in a let-down area for aircraft approaching either SFO or SJC."

"But that area doesn't show up on any of our navigational maps. How are we to know it's there?"

He told me the number of the chart that had that information on it and then asked if I had any other problems or questions. I did have the one last question.

"Why didn't a flight controller call me and warn me about the possibility of a close approach?"

"Well, I checked on that, too, and I was told that your IFF was not on or not operating. It seems that no one saw you." Oh.

Since it sounded as though he wasn't going to press the issue (for what reason I don't know...after all I was reporting a "near mid-air collision"), I meekly thanked him and hung up. Though I reported the non-operating IFF to maintenance, nothing more was ever said about the incident. Whew!

I searched around quite a bit before I could come up with the particular chart he had told me about, and, sure enough, there for all the world to see was a pie-shaped sector of California directly east of San Jose and southeast of San Francisco that was labeled as an aviation descent sector. A caution was given for aircraft to be diligent in flying through that area. Gee, thanks!

Asking around, I could find no one, not even the old timers, who knew about the let-down sector, and most didn't even know that there were special charts which depicted such sectors.

Well, as they say, "We live and learn." Or maybe it would better be said, "If we don't learn, we may not live."

Wise words from "The Preacher" (probably Solomon) in Ecclesiastes tell us that, *"No man knows when his hour may come...so men are trapped by evil times that fall unexpectedly upon them. No one knows what is coming..."* (Ecclesiastes 9:10 and 10:14 NIV)

I certainly didn't that day...and I was, once again, within seconds of exiting this life and entering into eternity. But this time, a multitude of others would have as well. It was not only an *honest* mistake, it took extensive research to even find out that it was a mistake. Honest or not, it could have cost hundreds their lives, and I think that was a great part of my emotion as I tried to wind down after everything was over.

Scores of people that day almost died, along with me. I know that I was spiritually prepared for the end of this life and entry into "Real Life" afterwards. That was proved several months later as I came even closer to death when the SAR aircraft I was in crashed in the Sierras directly below where we were practicing in-flight refueling that day of the near-miss.

But I just wonder about the multitude in the 747. We really *do* have to be ready...because, you see, they would have never known what hit them.

10.

LORD, HERE I COME!

For I am persuaded that neither death, nor life,
nor angels, nor principalities, nor powers,
nor things present, nor things to come,
nor height, nor depth, nor any other creature,
shall be able to separate us from the love of God,
which is in Christ Jesus our Lord.
Romans 8:38-39 KJV

Five years, nine months and some change after becoming the first aviator of the Vietnam war to be shot down and subsequently recovered from inland North Vietnam (twenty miles southeast of Hanoi, North Vietnam's capital), the same pilot once again experienced as close a brush with death as one might have and still be with us. Nearly six years earlier, having escaped an exploding aircraft a mere second or two before he would have been a part of its destruction, he was the only pilot rescued of the seven downed on September 20, 1965. The other six spent seven and one half years in torturous confinement as POWs. In this present crisis of July 2nd and 3rd, 1971, seven aviators—from three different crashes—were located, and only he was found alive. This is his—my—life and death story.

The events of July 2nd, 1971 were more concerned with death than life. Four men, three navy pilots and a civilian, were missing in a small plane in the rugged Sierra Nevada Mountains on a flight to Lake Tahoe. Since they had disappeared on 26 June, our search was, realistically, no longer for survivors, but for a crash site and four bodies. I had mentioned to Patty, my wife, how nearly impossible it was to spot a crash in the vast and remote Sierras. Later I was to regret having told her that.

At the time of this entire episode I was a Lieutenant Commander, US Navy, assigned to Air Wing Fifteen stationed at NAS Lemoore, California as the assistant Air Wing Landing Signal Officer. Having within the year reported from a two-year tour as a Company Officer at the U.S. Naval Academy, Patty and I had just been blessed with the birth of our daughter, Jennifer Cathleen, on May 30th.

God was in His heaven, and everything was right with the world...until the news of the missing plane came in on June 26th. One of the pilots in the missing aircraft was a former squadron mate of mine and the captain of the Naval Academy gymnastic team in 1962, the year before I graduated. I was saddened and scared and hopeful that the search-and-rescue activities would find them soon and alive.

By the time my name came up on the operations flight schedule for part of the SAR efforts on July 2nd, hope had pretty well given way to a realization that we most likely weren't going to find them alive. And then the grim task became simply trying to find the proverbial needle in the Sierras haystack.

The search planes available were tandem-seated, propeller-driven T28's. These planes were slower and less powerful than the jets that most of the pilots in the air group were flying. But, because of their greater "loiter time" (the ability to remain on station because of fuel considerations) than their fuel-gobbling cousins, and, because of their ability to fly lower and slower than the jets (thereby being able to search more thoroughly), these were the best aircraft for the mission. Since I was not yet checked out in the T28, I was going along only as a backseat observer, not really as a co-pilot.

The young pilot I was assigned was a quiet, efficient, and likeable officer just back from the war zone and only recently checked-out in the T28 himself. That was to loom large in the subsequent events of that day. But, not knowing how little time he had in the T28 (just the five required check flights, none of which were in the mountains) and, since I respected him and his abilities, I had no reason to think that this hop would be any different from any of the vast number of search missions which had preceded us.

The first two hours of the flight went reasonably well. Our search sector took us first over the rolling foothills northeast of Fresno, in the San Joaquin Valley, and then into the Sierras, up to the 10,000-foot level. The scenery would have been breathtakingly beautiful had the reason for the flight not been so tragically necessary. The high country, especially, was magnificent! But soon it became very, very deadly.

The only glitch in those first two hours was on one occasion when the pilot was flying us out of hilly country toward a ridgeline, and I wasn't really certain that we were going to clear the ridge. We did, and I felt somewhat like a backseat driver who wasn't hands-on in control and therefore didn't have the feel for the performance of the aircraft. So, I stopped worrying at that point.

As we began to reach our time and fuel points for turning toward home, we came out of a winding valley which made its way into a larger and very broad river plain. As we crossed the open area, Jim told me on the intercom that on our way home he'd like to investigate a fairly narrow canyon-like valley to our south that climbed up to a ridgeline across the end of it. As we flew into the entrance of the valley that rapidly sloped up on both sides and gently in front of us, Jim suddenly jammed the throttle fully forward. He'd forgotten to give us full power as we crossed the wide plain!

Had we been in one of our jets, we simply would have gone to 100% power, stood the aircraft on it's tail, climbed and rolled out at 15,000 feet with no problem. But this wasn't one of our jets, and it didn't take much in the way of assessment to realize that this airplane wasn't going to make it up over that ridgeline.

I looked to see what other options we had...perhaps a tight turn to get us out of there. But then it dawned on me; Jim had flown us up the lowest part of the valley, so that any turn in any direction required a climb...and we didn't have enough power to make both a climb and a turn, since turning always reduces the lift available. We had to continue straight ahead, hoping against hope that we would, in some way, be able to make it over the ridgeline. But long before we got there, it was apparent that we weren't going to clear the ridge. Since time was now standing still, I've never really been able to remember precisely how long I knew we were going to crash...it was somewhere in the range of one to two minutes, I believe. Slowly a flush crept over my face—the surest sign for me that my mind is telling my body to start the adrenalin flowing—something was about to happen!

I saw Jim remove the maps he had placed up on the console which were now restricting his vision out of the nose-high aircraft. He lowered the flaps to see if he could get a ballooning effect to gain more altitude. I looked out over the right wing, seeing the tall pine trees coming ever closer. Just then, I felt a slight bump. Of course, in an aircraft, that type of "slight" bump is usually catastrophic, as it was this time. Our left wing had been torn off by the top of a super-tall pine tree! I still have one of the post-accident photos of the wing up in that tree.

This was it! What had happened to the other guys we were searching for was about to happen to me...I was about to die! It's funny, but my life did not flash before my eyes; there was no tormented cry of "Why me, God? Why me?!"

"LORD, here I come!" A simple statement of fact, spoken aloud—quietly aloud—because I was assured that my God was mine and I was His, in death as well as in life.

And then we hit!

Having played four years of football in high school, I knew what hard knocks were. Having taken out a telephone pole with my car the previous March at 65 mph while trying to avoid a car which suddenly pulled out of a side road, I knew what a grinding, unyielding impact was. With over 350 carrier catapult shots and arrested landings under my belt, sudden starts and stops were no stranger to me. But absolutely nothing in my life had prepared me for the series of stunning, jolting shocks I experienced when we hit! There was no immediate pain associated with the contact, only a literal breathtaking, bruising, body-wracking continuum of jolts. Much like my ejection of several years before when I hit the air stream at 450 MPH, my mind was not really able to conceive of what was happening in hitting the mountain...until everything stopped. Back then everything had been quiet, and I had found myself floating peacefully down in a parachute. But this, this was quite a different story!

When everything stopped, I realized first that somehow I was still alive. That was a good start. I hoped to rest where I was (wherever that happened to be) for a few minutes to catch my breath and to get my bearings, but apparently I was not to have that luxury. As I opened my eyes, I saw flames already engulfing the front cockpit and licking over into mine. My first and greatest need at that point was to exit the cockpit.

Two important things had occurred in the crash that combined to save my life. The first was that, in hitting the tree with the left wing, it must have caused us to spiral down directly onto the *right* wing, which cushioned our contact in the boulder field to some degree as that wing broke off the plane and buckled under it. The post-accident photo of the plane looks as though the aircraft still had its *left* wing and was missing the *right* wing. However, the picture clearly shows the landing gear on that wing on the top, not the bottom, which clearly identifies the one wing remaining as the right wing, folded under the main body of the plane.

Of course, once again, that which was of benefit for me was not for Jim. Since the hollow wing is the main fuel tank for the plane, when it broke and folded under, it then spilled flaming aviation gasoline throughout Jim's cockpit and into mine.

Secondly, during the collision of the plane with the ground and the boulders, the wingless body of the plane came to rest nearly on its right side with the canopy shattered. Had the canopy stayed intact it is likely that I would not have made it out of the plane for a couple of reasons. The first was that, with the injuries I sustained in the crash, I wouldn't have been able to open the canopy, even had I known how. And the second was that I simply had not assumed that I would need to know how to open the canopy from the back seat... so I hadn't asked. That certainly could have been a stupidly fatal mistake.

Post-accident photo shows the right wing folded under the aircraft, as well as the burned out cockpit area. Note the binoculars used for searching on the rock next to the cockpit. (Official Navy Photograph)

As it was, seeing the flames just inches from my face, I quickly released my seatbelt and safety harness and half-crawled and half-fell out of the plane through the shattered canopy. I stood up only to discover to my dismay that I was not breathing…and I had no idea whether I could start to breathe. It was obvious that I had received a tremendous blow to my left chest area. Whatever the dynamics of the plane contacting the ground were, my entire left side had received the greater portion of the force and was completely incapacitated. I definitely had some broken ribs. My left knee and foot were hurting badly, probably broken; vision was almost zero out of my left eye from a combination of a blow to the head and cuts around my eye and nose (caused by my helmet visor having shattered and been forced down over my face).

As I continued to attempt to breathe again, I turned to look at Jim, to see if I could in some way assist him. When

I saw what I could of his cockpit (it was partially obscured by a boulder that his cockpit was resting against), my heart sank. His cockpit was fully engulfed in flames. In fact, I couldn't even see him.

The parachute, which was still attached to my harness, suddenly became too heavy for me, so I unhooked it and allowed it to fall to the ground. My mind kept telling me to do *something* to help Jim, and that it had to be *now*! There was only one thing wrong...I knew that I *couldn't* help him. I was still having difficulty just trying to breathe, and standing was rapidly becoming more than my body could take. The climb over the boulder to the cockpit was far beyond my physical capability.

As I collapsed to the ground there came an overwhelming sense of grief and frustration...because I realized clearly that, should I somehow be able summon the strength to make my way to his cockpit, the inferno raging there would not let me get close enough to do any good at all.

That's when I cried...and told Jim that I was sorry— sorry that I couldn't help him and sorry that I was alive and he wasn't. And that's when the question first flashed through my mind; not "Why me, LORD?" but, "Why *not* me, LORD?! Why Jim and not me?!"

That existential moment passed quickly as I heard two quick explosions coming from the engine or from Jim's cockpit. Jim at that time may have been beyond danger, but I certainly wasn't.

Still trying to begin breathing, I worked my way to my feet again and began to move away from the plane, up toward the ridgeline. After only a few steps I collapsed again and was then only able to propel myself away from the plane by sitting mainly on my right side, reaching out behind me with my right arm and hand and pulling myself forward, while at the same time pushing with my right leg and foot. It was slow and agonizing going, but soon I reached a site that I had noticed a couple hundred feet or so up the slope from the plane. That "scooting" remained my primary mobility for the rest of the time on the mountain.

At the site there was a huge boulder standing upright with a downed pine tree lying across in front of it with many branches broken off and scattered around. And, fifty feet or so off to the west, looking as though it had been placed there on purpose was a flat, somewhat circular boulder perched at the pinnacle of the ridge, giving an almost perfect 360 degree view to anyone standing or sitting on it. My first thought was that at least I'd be able to see planes coming from any direction looking for me. My second was that, if I had to spend the night, I would have a goodly amount of firewood available and a backdrop that would reflect the heat of a fire back to me.

The overhead photo of the crash site shows the almost-invisible aircraft (next to the lower part of the snow field), with the "fire site" and the "circular boulder" in the upper left. (Official Navy Photograph)

About then I began to experience some symptoms that I assumed were due to the injuries I had sustained and to the facts of my predicament...I was sure I was in some degree of shock. The most prominent of the symptoms was an overwhelming thirst. Though I had no water with me in the plane, I did have some plastic sandwich bags in my survival vest for just such an occasion.

I looked around and saw that, despite it being early summer, there were small fields of snow in the shadows of many of the boulders that kept the sun from sufficiently getting to them to melt the snow completely. So I slowly made my way down to the piles of snow, loaded up a couple of the bags, melting the snow by body heat, and subsequently filled both bags with water. I drank some then, replenished the bags, and took them back up to the fire site for drinking during the night should I not be found that day.

For the next few hours I either sat on the edge of the circular boulder or laid down in the volcanic ash-based dirt when I couldn't stay upright, listening and looking for rescue aircraft (or really any aircraft that I might be able to attract with my signal mirror). Since we were not provided with emergency radios, no one really knew where we were (except having our assigned search sector and our likely routes to and from the base). Though I saw a number of commercial aircraft, they were far too high to be able to spot a signal-mirror flash.

However, late in the afternoon I heard a plane coming from the south (I was sitting on the boulder facing north). Since adjusting my position in any way was terrifically painful and had to be done agonizingly slowly, by the time I eased around to be able to see the plane, it was in a turn, directly over me. Even though it was not more than perhaps fifteen hundred feet above me and I was able to get my signal mirror focused directly on it, all I saw was the bottom and then the tail end of the plane. They were looking for me and almost found me. But that was the last plane of the day.

Now I had to plan the night and my future actions. I was certain they would be out looking for us, just as we had been for the other downed aircraft. So, I decided to give them all of the next day before I even thought of more drastic actions. After all, I knew they were searching; as best I knew my injuries were not life threatening; and the only other things I could think of doing could be dangerous to me as well as to many others. I thought briefly of starting enough of a fire to really attract attention. But, starting a forest fire with no ability to control it was necessarily going to be a dangerous and very last-ditch effort.

So, using the abundance of dry wood around, the tree that was lying across in front of the tall boulder, and the small store of matches in my survival vest, I started a nice fire that I was pretty certain I could sustain through the night. With enough warmth and enough water, I was reasonably comfortable under the conditions…as long as I didn't sneeze, cough, or laugh. Though lying still was almost impossible because of the pain, I was nearly able to get to sleep a couple of times during the night.

As dawn slowly approached, I made my greatest mistake during the whole episode…I allowed my fire to go out, assuming the sun would soon warm me up. Wrong! Whoever said, "The night is coldest just before the dawn," knew precisely what he was talking about. Though it was light for at least an hour before the sun actually cleared the Sierras to my east, the warmth of the sun wasn't there and, in my weakened and pain-wracked state, my body temperature began to plummet. My thought during this whole time was to be certain not to miss a plane as I had the afternoon before…but I very much traded safety (the warmth of the fire) for hope (the sighting of a rescue plane).

As it turned out, I needn't have bothered. While sitting on the boulder shivering, once again I heard a plane coming from behind me, and once again, before I could get around to see it, it was over me and going away from me to the north. As disappointed as I was in missing it, I had a very deep conviction that it would return in a couple of hours, and that that was the plane that would find me. The profound sense of the presence of God, which was the legacy of my having been shot down and recovered from North Vietnam six years before, was standing me in good stead during this present struggle. Though my prayer was that I would be found sooner rather than later, I felt very strongly that whatever I had to go through during this present crisis would in fact once again strengthen my faith and deepen my trust in God's constant presence and love.

So, I sat there on the boulder, slowly and agonizingly moving myself around, trying to be prepared to signal to any aircraft that might come my way. Besides my signal mirror, I had a "pencil flare gun." Fitting easily into one of the pockets on my flight suit, this little apparatus fired small, one-inch sized flares that simply had a brief flare life followed by a small smoke trail...but, it was better than nothing.

Sure enough, at about 9:00 a.m. (almost precisely two hours after passing over me heading north), the T-28 was approaching on its way home. This time I was facing the right way. Quickly pulling out my little flare gun, I fired a flare and then honed in on the cockpit of the approaching T-28 with my mirror. Although it looked as though it was simply going to fly by to the west, it slowly began a turn back to me. As it approached, it began to waggle its wings! I was found!

Later, the back-seat observer in that plane, a good friend of mine who lived only a few blocks from Patty and me, told me about the morning. When he had passed our house at about 5:00 a.m. on his way to the base and seeing the lights on, he almost stopped to tell Patty that he was going to find me. Then, after searching their sector for a couple of hours and getting low on fuel, they were heading home when the pilot suddenly said, "Did you see that?" My friend said, "What?" and the pilot answered, "I thought I saw a flash of light." My friend said, "No, but I thought I saw a trail of smoke," and that's when they turned back to check. Praise God! I thought it of interest that my friend said that neither of them could hold back from weeping when they found me.

Fortunately for them and for me, a helicopter was already airborne. They were dangerously low on fuel, but they didn't want to leave me until the helo was close by. So, as the helo approached they were able to head home to safety. While we awaited the helo, I rotated around the boulder as they were circling me, keeping my mirror directly on their cockpit...I was not taking any chances that they would somehow lose sight of my position.

I heard the helo approaching, and soon I saw a paramedic coming from around the ridge. The helo had found a place to set down about a quarter of a mile away. As it turned out, the second most dangerous and terrifying part of the whole episode was about to begin.

The paramedic checked on me and saw that I was alive and responsive. He asked about the pilot, and I told him that I was certain he was killed in the crash and the subsequent fire. He went down and checked on Jim and confirmed that. He then called for the helo to lower a litter.

As the helo approached and hovered over us the paramedic and I lost communication because of the noise of the helo. The litter came down and the paramedic had me to lie down in it and then strapped me in with a strap across my waist and one across my ankles and then one across my chest. As he cinched down the strap across my chest, he pulled it as tight as possible right across my broken ribs. I know he was trying to ensure that I was safely strapped in. Nevertheless, it hurt like the dickens, and I yelled at him to stop, fearing that he would shatter the broken ribs and puncture a lung. But he just couldn't hear me, and I couldn't move my arms or hands to signal to him. But that wasn't the worst that was to happen.

The litter was supposed to have two lanyards from it attached to the single line coming down from the helo. The lanyard from the head of the litter was shorter than the one from the foot, so that the litter was raised up to the helo at about a thirty-degree angle, head high. That was to allow the crewman in the helo simply to pull the litter directly into the helo hatch before he lowered it to the deck of the helo.

That was the way it was *supposed* to work. Unfortunately, reality didn't quite match the plan. The lanyard from the foot of the litter was broken. So when the helo began to winch the litter up, the litter was pulled up vertically, not at the thirty-degree angle. By itself that was not a terrible problem, since the paramedic *had* cinched me in *very tightly*. Where the problem arose was that, due to the swirling winds caused by the helo's rotating blades, the lanyard attached to the line pulling me up wrapped itself around my neck, and I was being pulled up and choked at the same time. Once again, no one could hear my cries...except me, and I knew what was wrong.

When I finally was up at the hatch of the helo, the crewman unwrapped the lanyard from around my neck. He then rotated the litter so that I was facing away from him and then started to pull it into the helo. There was only one problem. Since the litter was hanging straight up and down and not at the thirty-degree angle from the horizontal as it was supposed to be, the litter hit the top and bottom of the hatch opening and wouldn't fit in. So, the crewman then wrapped his arms around the litter and me and began pulling with all his might to get me in. In doing so, he was pulling once again right across my broken ribs. Once again I screamed, "Stop! Stop! You're going to shatter my ribs!" But, of course, he couldn't hear me.

Just then the helo began to move and flew to the site where they had let the paramedic out. When the helo set down, I sighed in relief...at least now the crewman would get out and lift my litter in properly so that he wouldn't kill me. Once again, WRONG! The pilots had moved to where they could land *to protect the crewman so that he wouldn't fall out while trying to get the litter into the helo!* All he did at that point was to set his feet better and began again to pull me into the helo, once again across my broken ribs. Still none of my screams could be heard!

Finally, with one last desperate pull across my broken ribs, he pulled so hard that the metal litter actually bent sufficiently for it to fit in the hatch. By this time I was sure I was dead...or I wished that I were!

As we began to head back to Lemoore, the terrific pain began slowly to subside, and I found that, once more, I was still alive...against all odds. You can be certain that I detailed the well-intentioned but near-fatal procedures of the paramedic and the aircrew of the helo in my after-action report.

When we landed, Patty and my mom (who was visiting and helping Patty with our baby) were on hand as I was off-loaded, put on a gurney and rushed into the ER. This was my first (and so far only) time to see what it was like having everyone looking down at you as you were wheeled along for medical treatment.

After a complete check, all were amazed that, other than the broken parts, in general I was in very good shape. In fact, the things that were broken couldn't be or didn't need to be put in a cast (the ribs and the foot were simply wrapped in order to keep them from moving too much). The left knee was severely bruised but not broken. However, it had no spring to it for the next decade, though the ability to jump did return slowly. The cuts around my nose and eye were not too serious, and a cut down to the bone on my left leg couldn't be stitched because of the passage of too much time. So, for the next month or so, it simply had to be cleaned out a couple of times a day to allow it to heal from the inside out.

As it turned out, I got to see all of both sides of our families during this particular adventure. When my mom heard that I was missing, she immediately called my brother, who flew out from North Carolina. Patty's family (mom, dad, and two younger sisters who were still in school and at home) were already driving on their way from Maryland to see Baby Jenny and couldn't be located on the highway by the State Patrol. So, when they arrived the next day, the first thing they heard was that I had been in a plane crash and was in the hospital.

When they came to the hospital to visit me, something rather unusual occurred. The nurse had come in to give me a shot for the pain before they were allowed in the room. As they entered my room, I began to feel somewhat peculiar and then kind of out of it. It wasn't at all unpleasant. I don't know whether they could tell that I was a bit spacey, or if they just thought it was the result of the crash. Later, after the family had left, the nurse returned very apologetically and told me that she had accidentally given me twice the amount of pain-killer she was supposed to have. Right then I saw the attraction of recreational drugs. During their whole visit, I had been off in happy land…floating about a foot off the bed.

Since there was very little that the hospital staff could do for me there that couldn't be done at home, I was discharged after three days and given a regimen for allowing the healing of the broken parts and the cuts and bruises. After a couple of months of recuperation, I was given a flight physical and was pronounced fit for a return to flight status.

On that Fourth of July weekend, three crashes and seven aviators were found…the plane we were looking for which had crashed in a thunderstorm in the mountains short of Lake Tahoe, Jim and me, and a jet pilot who had disappeared the previous December. I was the only one found alive. This time the question was, "Why me, LORD, why me? Why was I protected?" Once again I have no answer.

My position as the assistant Air Wing LSO had been

turned over to someone else, so I was assigned to an A-7E squadron flying the navy's newest attack jet, the Corsair II. I was assigned as the Safety Officer and was sent to the Naval Aviation Safety School at Monterey, California. Afterwards, I was promoted to the third ranking officer in the squadron and became the Maintenance Officer. But during that time, I began to realize that my competency as a high-performance-jet aviator had taken quite a hit by my most recent brush with death coupled with the more distant one in Vietnam. I began making small mistakes that I knew I shouldn't be making. And I began to realize that those small mistakes could ultimately kill me...and, as the third ranking officer in the squadron, I would always have at least one, and many times three, other aircraft on my wing. If I pulled a stupid and killed myself, there would then be three other holes in the ground right next to mine. I couldn't see that happening.

Thus, in the summer of 1972 I requested to be removed from flight status, and asked to return to the Naval Academy as an instructor (since I had a letter from the Academy in my personnel files which stated that I had grades sufficiently high to allow me to return to instruct in chemistry, engineering, or fluid mechanics). I was sent back as a chemistry instructor for the 1972-73 Academic Year. It was wonderful to be back in association with the Academy, the Brigade of Midshipmen, and Patty's folks, who still lived in Annapolis.

But, after doing my best to find a career pattern that would provide me with a serious challenge and that I could see would be of value for the navy, it became apparent that the navy really didn't know what to do with an ex-aviator. Their best shot was to put me on a carrier division staff as an assistant maintenance officer where I would spend a year at a time in the western Pacific shifting from carrier to carrier doing the thing I disliked the most, dealing with the maintenance portion of aviation.

That was when Patty and I realized that, as much as we

would have loved to have had the benefits of retirement from the navy, we simply couldn't see staying in a dead-end career pattern assigned to positions that, not only did I not like, but in which I was really not competent. Plus, we really didn't feel that marking time until retirement and my missing out on Jenny's years 2 to 12 would be a wise use of our next decade as a family.

So, in August of 1973 I left active duty, and after a few years as a Navy Blue and Gold Officer (a public relations and field-evaluation officer for the Naval Academy), I found that I could retire (but without benefits) under a special, little-known provision which allowed officers to be listed as "retired" who had reached a particular age and who had been wounded in combat. Since my dad had been a 20-year navy man, and, since I had given fourteen active duty years to the navy (Naval Academy time doesn't count toward retirement, but I had entered when I was seventeen and I left the navy when I was thirty-one), and, finally, since I had nearly given my life on two occasions (and scared myself witless on several others), I wanted to maintain my link to the navy, even though I got none of the benefits I would have had at retirement after twenty years of active duty service.

To finish this account of my second "near death experience of the most tangible kind," I would like to quote from some edited excerpts of a letter I wrote to all of my high school classmates after our Fortieth-Year Class Reunion (in 1999). Though I was unable to attend the reunion, I had reports of it sent from various friends and discovered that precisely 10% of the class was by then deceased. Here is, in part, what I said to them:

Dear Classmates,

Shortly before his death in 1964, General Douglas MacArthur made a very moving and impassioned speech to the assembled Corps of Cadets at West Point, his alma mater and where he had subsequently been the Superintendent. He concluded his talk with this:

In my dreams I hear again the crash of guns, the rattle of musketry, the strange, mournful mutter of the battlefield. But in the evening of my memory always I come back to West Point. Always there echoes and re-echoes: Duty, Honor, Country.

Today marks my final roll call with you. But I want you to know that when I cross the river, my last conscious thoughts will be of the Corps, and the Corps, and the Corps. I bid you farewell.

Although I had the privilege of attending the United States Naval Academy at Annapolis, I'm certain that "when I cross the river" my final thoughts will not be "...of the Brigade, and the Brigade, and the Brigade."

Folks, we're in the autumn of our years. The early spring of our lives in '55-'59 was exciting, and I trust that you've experienced all that you dreamed about when we were on the other side of adulthood. But now it is starting to get late for us. Some of us won't be here to reunite for our 45th. Many more may not be here for the 50th. There are some vital questions about life that need to be addressed before then. And, so, I'm going to do so now.

I had the misfortune (or the "good fortune") to experience "my last conscious thoughts" and to say my "last words" upon this earth nearly three decades ago. I was in the back seat of a search-and-rescue aircraft looking for a downed plane in the Sierra Nevada Mountains. My pilot made a mistake and flew us into a ridgeline at about 10,000 feet. As the plane broke apart going through some tall pine trees and we spun down into a boulder field, my last words (said out loud...I know, because I badly bit both sides of my tongue when we hit) were, "LORD, here I come!" I had no reason to expect to live through the crash. The pilot sitting about five feet in front of me was killed, and I was badly injured...but here I am.

My last thoughts were not of the Brigade of Midshipmen, were not of Pineville High, and were not even of my young bride of eight years, the love of my life, nor of my infant daughter, the light of my life. My last thoughts were of the reality of eternity and of the God whom I had loved and served since I was eight years old and who had guided my life through the bright times and the dark, whose hand had led me and whose right hand had held me (Psalm 139:7-10) when I was shot down over North Vietnam and during other life-threatening events in and out of aviation. And I'm trusting that when He does finally call me home, my final thoughts will repeat those of July 2, 1971 and my final words will echo again, "LORD, here I come!"

My prayer for each of you who reads *Wings of the Morning* is that you will never have to experience a life or death situation such as the one I lived through thirty-five years ago in July of 2006. And, as well, I pray that you will have settled in your own heart and life the reality of our mortality on this earth and the eternal existence that we will then experience when our time on this earth comes to an end.

And may we all then join in chorus together, "LORD, here I come!"

finis

Printed in the United States
47447LVS00002B/217-339